Edited by Jane E. Stahl and Susan Biebuyck
Volume Four
Printed in 2017

R. R. Bowker - US ISBN Agency
ISBN: 978-0-9788838-7-4 0-9788838-8-8

Cover Illustration entitled "Scribble" by Jim Meehan

PREFACE

Muse: The Inspirations of Our Lives

"We can do no great things, but we can do small things with great love." ~Mother Teresa

"Words are small things, but the right words, at the right moment, have power to inspire or degrade, heal or wound, champion or discourage. Their power is felt among all of us at any age or stage or position throughout our lives. Words can transform our lives and the lives of others."

*****

These were the words I used to introduce a writing assignment to my high school sophomores. I imagined that they might recall advice like my father often gave me to inspire my courage before an athletic event or vocal performance. "Give 'em hell, Kiddo!" was his favorite send-off.

I thought some might recall their mother's words at a turning point in their lives, words that clarified a decision, offered comfort, or provided some understanding. Perhaps they'd recall a line of poetry, a slogan from an advertisement or song lyric that had resonated with them.

My hope was that in sharing the stories of how words had influenced their lives, they would realize their own power through the use of well-chosen words—words with the power to be a supporting actor in someone else's life story—words that gave someone else's life story a happy ending or the encouragement to "carry on."

Through this assignment, I learned what motivated my students and what they valued. This intimate glimpse into their young minds and hearts created an opportunity to enhance our work together while inspiring me with their wisdom and compassion.

Two books inspired the assignment: Marlo Thomas's book entitled <u>The Right Words at the Right Time</u> contained revelations from more than 100 celebrated men and women of our time who shared a moment when words changed their lives.

Her book includes the stories from leaders, celebrities and sports figures like Mohammed Ali, Tom Brokaw, Steven Spielberg, Toni Morrison, Jack Nicholson, Laura Bush, Billy Crystal, Katie Couric, Al Pacino, Chris Rock, and Ruth Bader Ginsburg. The stories they told provided a window into their lives, their values, and their character.

The second book is a work by Robert Fulghum entitled <u>Words I Wish I Wrote</u>, a collection of words and phrases that he loved from writers such as Jerry Garcia, Albert Camus, Dylan Thomas, and Franz Kafka. I found many of my own favorites among his.

Thus, the original intent was for our area's writers to share stories from their lives of words that had inspired them. And the challenge to our artists was to represent visually a person, place, or thing that had inspired their art.

As in many endeavors, however, things don't always turn out as planned. In the case of our current volume of poetry and prose, a number of our local writers preferred the visual artist's challenge and shared through their words what people, places, things, ideas—and sometimes words—had inspired their lives.

The diversity of genre and writing style, as well as the varied subjects evoking their inspiration, has created a happy change to the original plan! I think you will agree and be inspired as well!

~jane stahl

TABLE OF CONTENTS

Artist: Susan Biebuyck, Photograph,"Faking Bitch Face"

THE TRUTH ABOUT DOGS

*Note: The following story is an excerpt from an unpublished manuscript titled: **The Piano Room***

A few years before they took Cook away, brother Earl and Cook's half-brother, Jerry, decided to abandon our baseball game and head through the woods to Sam the Hubcap Man's house, without the two tag-a-longs, Cook and me.

Objecting fiercely, Cook shouted, "Why can't we come along? We were good enough to play baseball with!"

"Because we said so," the older boys said in unison. Earl and Jerry were three years older than Cook and I.

Of course, that would make sense to a little sister, who was used to being hammered on and illogically responded to, but it was not a reasonable excuse for Cook. Maybe it was his emerging frustration with his not belonging—not wanted at his home, not belonging to our home, and not really being a brother to Jerry. Whatever, Cook was pissed.

"Come on!" Cook spit out, as he grabbed my sleeve and yanked me toward the wooded path. "We're going, too."

"No, I can't go. We don't know the way. We'll get lost," I pleaded. The path to Sam's was forbidden fruit territory, far beyond where my trembling ten-year-old legs had voluntarily ventured. I just knew if we went, there'd be trouble.

"Earl and Jerry will kill us," I muttered as we started running after them.

Soon we nearly caught up with them, disregarding their boy-imagined threats of violence. Cook was determined to be part of this adventure. I knew I shouldn't be there and certainly didn't belong.

Suddenly, out of nowhere, came a blur of barking dogs, about fifty yards to the rear. They were quickly closing in. I didn't recognize the dogs as members of the neighborhood pack of misfits, nor did they seem intent on making our acquaintance.

At that moment we all realized the danger and started screaming and running as fast as our adolescent legs could carry us. Our older brothers took the lead, completely ignoring their younger siblings and our frantic pleas for help.

"Cook! Look. The dogs . . . they are getting closer . . . they are going to eat us!" I yelled, tears streaming down my cheeks, horrified, as I caught sight of the barking beasts and nearly tripping.

"Run, run fast!" Cook frantically puffed, as the boys in front increased their lead.

"Help! Help us, Earl," I pleaded, both of us now crying, stumbling as we ran up the twisting, rock-covered trail.

Just then, almost in synchrony, Cook and I tripped on a branch and flew forward, landing terrified on our tearing faces.

"Oh, no . . . the dogs. They're gonna get us," screamed Cook, looking back at the snarling pack bearing down toward us.

I reached my hand out to grab Cook's shaking hand--crying, squeezing his hand, and bravely awaiting our fate.

It seemed an eternity had passed waiting for the inevitable snapping teeth, the tearing of flesh, and the pain. In those death-anticipating moments where even young lives flash like memory meteorites, I wondered out loud, "Why are you doing this?"

All I heard in response was that sinister chuckle, a laugh that would haunt my mind for years along with the unanswered question, "Why'd you do it": For years I could never fathom why or how he could leave me to be taken by the dogs? What kind of brother leaves his sister to die in such a manner. Why did you do it, Earl?

Cook and I survived the dogs that day. When we fell, we no longer were part of the chase. The dogs closed in on us, leaped over the branch we had tripped on, dodged our bodies that lie motionless awaiting our fate, and ran barking after our brothers who were chased clear to Sam's sanctuary in the woods, which I never did find via that path, at least on that day.

That day I learned two heard-earned lessons – the truth about dogs and a bittersweet truth about my brother.

~Claudia J. Bahorik

Claudia Bahorik, M.S., P.T., D.O., is currently reinventing herself as a Professional Writing Student at Penn State Berks Campus. Having retired last spring as a family physician, Dr. Bahorik has been involved in writing in one form or another for most of her professional career. She is a writer for <u>The Merchandiser,</u> *a weekly local newspaper, and was previously published in* <u>Country Magazine</u>, *as a ghost writer for a short story told by her mother. She is currently working on a paranormal romance titled "The Seventh Ghost" - a story based on unusual happenings on her Berks County farm.*

Artist: Susan Fellows, Acrylic on canvas, "Three of Mugs"

PROPHETIC WORDS

In Gratitude to My First Spiritual Teacher Ray Bozeman

"You are destined to be a healer!" the tall, gentle, bear-of-a-man exclaimed to me as we met for the third and final day in San Francisco. I could not even comprehend the weight of the words he spoke. I did not know what they meant for a long time. I was only twenty-four years old.

As I was preparing to leave the City of Saint Francis after spending nine transformative months living and working to "find myself" as a young gay man, Ray Bozeman walked down the basement stairs of Stacey's Bookstore to find me in the paperback book department where I was working.

I looked up from shelving books to find Ray's huge, blissful figure moving towards me. I stood up to greet him as he sounded with great urgency, "Spirit told me that you were leaving the city and I needed to see you." Astonished, I thought How could he know that I was leaving? Ray continued, "Would you meet with me the next few days in the city?" Of course, I responded affirmatively.

I had met this extraordinary, kind, thirty-something gay man through my new housemates, Ken Barnard, Jerry "Pickles" Henderson, and Stephen B. Cass, who called themselves "gay white witches" from the border town of Bristol, Virginia, and Tennessee. We visited Ray in the old hotel he lived in on Polk Street. That day he was dressed in a white Egyptian-style robe wearing a King Tut-like headdress, which reminded me of Batman's and Robin's nemesis on the 1960s TV show.

I learned that day that Ray took in the young gay males who had been thrown out of their parents' homes and were living on the streets of San Francisco working as prostitutes to survive. He provided them food, shelter, and a safe place to be. I could feel his abiding love for them as he spoke and introduced some of them on our visit.

That was the last time I had seen Ray until he came to Stacey's Bookstore. For three days, he and I were inseparable: walking, eating, and being together before I flew back to my hometown of Bethlehem, PA, on the East Coast.

When we walked through the closely-cropped trees of San Francisco City Hall one night, Ray advised, "Do not be afraid of the darkness, Michael. You are safe and protected here. Nothing will harm you."

I was stunned in response. I had grown up being afraid at night in the dark. As a child, I always felt as if some bogey man or being would come to get me and take me away. I thought Ray knows something about me that I never shared with him as he revealed his teaching to me.

I did not fully comprehend why Ray wanted to spend this time with me. All I knew was that I trusted him. He was a gentle and kind soul. In all honesty, I did not understand what he was saying to me. So when he said those prophetic words, "You are destined to be a healer!" on our last day together, they did not compute.

Months earlier, my housemate Stephen, taking a much-needed mental health day off from work as a responsible hospital administrator, invited me into his bedroom. He delightfully shared his knowledge and deck of Aleister Crowley Thoth tarot cards. Stephen spread the large symbolic cards with powerful visuals on his bedcover. I had never witnessed a tarot deck. Again, I did not understand what he was talking about or what they meant. But as with Ray, I felt that Stephen was a kind and loving gay man. I felt safe with him and what he was conveying.

I said goodbye to Ray and San Francisco, not realizing how important this journey had been. When I started working for Mrs. Anna Rodale, widow of J.I. Rodale, founder of Rodale Press, at her South Bethlehem Ann Ar Book Shoppe, I spotted the large Aleister Crowley Thoth deck in the showcase. Something clicked! In that moment, intuitively, I made my decision to study the Tarot directly with Spirit. I had always felt close with God and the angels as a child. My maternal Poppy spoke to the spirits and the dead to heal the family curse, the unusual accidents and deaths occurring.

For nine years, I studied intuitive Tarot directly in relationship with Spirit. Now, for twenty-eight years, I have served Spirit as Blue Turtle, intuitive counselor and teacher. It took many years for me to realize and recognize that Ray Bozeman had been my first spiritual teacher. In San Francisco in 1979, he spoke to me about my future life and work as Blue Turtle. I am grateful that Spirit led Ray to guide me to understand "You are destined to be a healer!" It is my greatest joy and fulfillment to serve as an instrument of Spirit.

~Rev. Michael Barnett, M.Div., M.Ed.

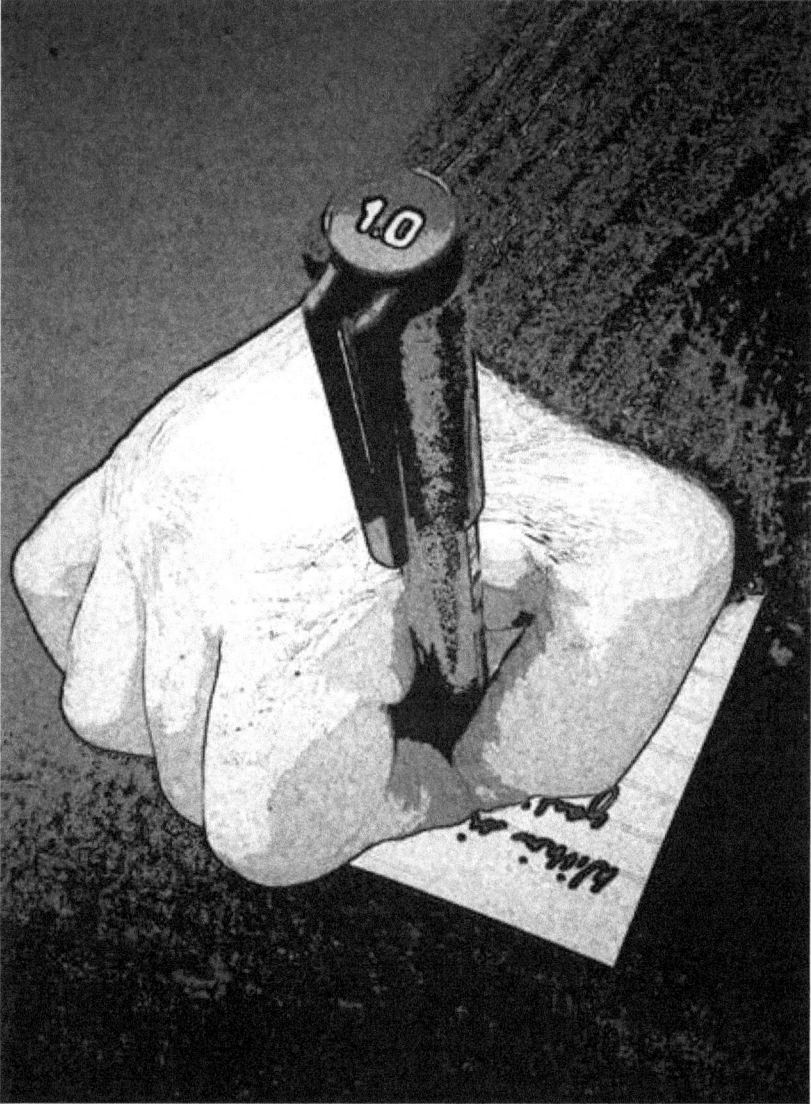

Artist: Susan Biebuyck, Digital iPhone art, "Automatic Handwriting"

Automatic Handwriting Words

*In Gratitude to My Past Life Native
Great-Great-Great-Grandmother Nonah Berah*

"Within six years, you'll be moving to the Southwest to do healing work!" I never anticipated receiving this insight through my Native American great-great-great-grandmother from a past life. In late October 1986, I was washing my laundry in the basement of my apartment building in Northern Liberties neighborhood of Philadelphia, PA. Suddenly, I started receiving automatic handwriting that I immediately wrote down.

I was Brown Bear, a member of this native tribe located in the upper Midwest of the United States. Through my mind's eye, I watched my mother and sister being killed by enemy warriors from another tribe while our warriors, including my father, were out hunting. My younger brother and I watched in silent horror as we hid in the pile of animal skins and furs under the worktable.

Then I met our tribal elders as they assessed my spiritual progress and development. We retreated into a mountain cave where I was initiated in the water as a young warrior. As the tears flowed from my eyes, I watched my pen automatically write through the voice of my great-great-great grandmother, "Within six years, you'll be moving to the Southwest to do healing work!"

When I rationally assessed this unique occurrence with my mind, it just did not connect with my current life and circumstances. I tucked this "letter" from my great-great-great grandmother away for a future time and continued my current life.

Lo and behold! Over these nearly six years, my whole life changed! New friends invited me to drive with them to the Southwest in their van to visit Sedona, Arizona, then on to Santa Fe, New Mexico, where other new friends from Philadelphia had moved. Initially, I declined. Then I remembered the "letter."

I wanted to live in Sedona, but Spirit said, "You cannot live in a nurturing garden," and pointed out on the map through me the Glorieta/Pecos area twenty miles SW of Santa Fe where I was to live. I did not want to live near Santa Fe, but I found a lovely casita on the Koch farm in Glorieta and surrendered to Spirit.

Once settled in Glorieta, I began my psychic handwriting analysis and intuitive tarot readings at Trader Jack's Outdoor Flea Market near Santa Fe in Tesuque Pueblo. The automatic handwriting words, "Within six years, you'll be moving to the Southwest to do healing work!" from my great-great-great-grandmother came true! By word-of-mouth, I have been doing my Blue Turtle Intuitive Counseling for 28 years. I was open to Spirit in my life and completely surrendered in total trust to the Divine.

~Rev. Michael Barnett, M.Div., M.Ed.

Rev. Michael Barnett, M.Div., M.Ed. works as Blue Turtle, Intuitive Counselor, for 28 years serving the metaphysical community. He comes from an intuitive maternal Serbian-Croatian (Middle Eastern-Ashkenazi) - Ukrainian (Central Asian-Caucasus) lineage. Blue Turtle's messages from Mother of Light, Grandfather Shaman of Mesa Verde, Shockara Starbeings, and Mahatma Gandhi are published in Sedona Journal of Emergence. His Mystery School of Emerging Eternity in small groups is in its third year. Blue Turtle's intuitive narratives for the photographs "Door" and "Sink" by Dan R. Talley in his series, "Seeing Through Psychics," were part of the exhibition, "Allentown X 7: Photographic Explorations," at the Allentown Art Museum of the Lehigh Valley from November 13, 2016 through February 5, 2017.

DISHWASHER PETE

Sometime not terribly long ago (I have no recollection of where, when, or from whom), I heard about the words of an individual apparently known only as "Dishwasher Pete." Dishwasher Pete is reputed to have said, "My old man worked hard all his life till he was seventy years old just so he could sit on the porch and do nothin'. Hell, I can do that now." For some reason those words have stayed with me ever since. Pete's father certainly sounds like not only an outstanding example of delayed gratification *ad infinitum* but also someone whose apparent dedication to hard work and its attendant virtues we are all encouraged to emulate. Yet such an aberration from man's natural inclinations brings to mind a few additional words that have remained with me and always will. They are uttered by Anthony Quinn in the role of Zorba the Greek in the mid-sixties film based on Nikos Kazantzakis' novel.

"You know, Boss," Zorba says, his tone more sympathetic than accusatory; "you have everything. Everything but one thing."

"Wha... What's that?" the Boss asks hesitantly.

"Madness. A man needs a little madness. Otherwise, he never really dares to cut the rope... and be free!"

I actually read Kazantzakis' book—twice—before I got around to watching the movie many years after it had been made. And, much to my consternation, when I looked for some of my favorite lines from the movie in the translation of Zorba that I owned at the time, I was unable to locate them. It was apparently a simple matter of difference between the translation of the novel and the screenplay that had been based upon it, but the same ideas that had so intrigued me when I read the novel seemed to be expressed much more directly and succinctly in the dialogue of the film script.

However, regardless of whether it happened to be in Greek or in English, in a novel or in a screenplay, the content of the observation was the same; and its general theme was one that is encountered frequently in the notable literature of our time. The conversation, for example, could easily be seen as a slight variation on the one that took place between Doc Daneeka and Captain Yossarian early in Joseph Heller's

<u>Catch-22</u>. Madness. Freedom. Are they really that closely related? Is the former really the only way to achieve the latter in the world we've created for ourselves?

Many of us would shake our heads and frown at the obvious immaturity, irresponsibility, short-sightedness, and sloth of Dishwasher Pete. "He must be nuts," we would say to ourselves. "What about his future? How can he waste his potential like that? Where will he be in another twenty or thirty years?" But how many of us would also admit to a twinge of envy for someone with the courage to shuck the yoke and thumb his nose at convention; to be his own, true self even at the expense of becoming an outlier to the bell curve of society's expectations; or, as Zorba had put it, "to cut the rope... and be free"?

~ *Craig Bennett*

Craig H. Bennett, author of <u>Nights on the Mountain</u>, <u>A Spiritual Journey</u> holds degrees from Ursinus and Johns Hopkins. He has a substantial background in music, has worked as a professional on-camera and voice-over performer in Philadelphia and New York, and is retired from the faculty of Valley Forge Military College. He has traveled extensively in Europe, visited the former Soviet Union, and participated in an expedition to the dry tropical wilderness of northeastern Brazil on the trail of Col. Percival H. Fawcett, who disappeared in 1925 while searching for the lost city he designated as "Z."

FIRE FUCKING ISLAND

My family has always loved to travel; we have had the most extravagant vacations around the world. However, there is one vacation I will never forget. When I was about nine years old and summer was nearing its end, we were looking for one last fun vacation to take before school started. We wanted something that was still going be relatively close by. At the time, I had a baby sitter who was a long-time family friend. She recommended Fire Island to us. She claimed that her family had an amazing time there and that she was looking forward to going back the next summer. My family also loves bicycling, and she explained that Fire Island was perfect for bicycling because cars were not permitted on the island, making the bike everyone's main form of transportation. It seemed like a perfect place for us. So, my mom, dad, and I drove several hours to get to the ferry that was supposed to take us directly to our hotel on the island. Our troubles began when, despite my warning, we got on the wrong boat.

Unfortunately, the boat dropped us at the opposite side of the island. We were forced to drag our heavy suitcases through the hot sand to our hotel. My parents hoped and claimed that when we got to the hotel and could finally rent bikes, things would be fun. Once we finally arrived, the staff explained that our room wouldn't be ready for several hours because they didn't clean it in time. Angry, we were starving and decided to ask where to get food. The hotel staff said that places to eat were at the other side of the island where we were dropped off. We decided to go rent bikes so it would not be such a terrible trip back for food. Unfortunately, ALL the bikes were rented for the season except for one without a seat. However, we began walking towards the food anyway because I felt like I was going to pass out. I was young, and it had already been a long, strenuous day. I was exhausted and began to cry. My dad walked off, annoyed and cursing, not at me or my mom, but just that the vacation was turning out to be horrible. My mom and I sat down and shared the last drops of her water. We are both very Nordic, so we burn very easily. Our skin was bright red and hot to the touch. The sun beat down on us and shade was impossible to find. I will never forget how hot it felt that day. As we sat there, upset and weakened from the heat in the one hundred degree weather, we noticed a man riding up on a tandem, without anyone on the back. "That's strange," I thought. "Wait! I recognize him!" I said.

It was my dad! I looked up at him on the tandem as he rode closer. He was my hero in that moment. There were no bikes left on this island; and yet somehow, in a matter of about twenty minutes, he appeared with the most amazing, beautiful bike. It was a light blue, beach cruiser tandem that had thick wheels too that maneuvered easily through the sand.

He said, "Come on Edie, we will grab food while Mom finally checks us into the hotel!" My mom was so proud of him and called him "Super Gavin" as we always do. We rode away in search for food and water. As I sat on the back of the tandem comfortably having my dad do ninety percent of the pedaling, I felt like I was with a rockstar. The wind in our hair cooled us as we moved forward.

I asked, "Dad, how did you find this amazing tandem bike that's so pretty?"

He said, "Oh yaa knoooow… I just took it." "

WHAT?" I exclaimed.

My heart immediately began to race; I was so enraged. "How could he?" I thought. I told him to stop riding and demanded that he give me his phone so I could call Mom. I started to sob as the phone rang. She finally answered, and I hyperventilated while saying, "MOM, Dad stole this tandem bike; we are all going to go to jail!"

She comforted me and said it was fine because she saw a sign on the back of the bike that said "PROPERTY OF PALMS HOTEL," the only other hotel on the island. She told me we would not get arrested. I could not believe she believed that! I thought in that second that both my parents were filthy criminals. After her talking to me for about fifteen minutes, I began to calm down and collect myself. I was still very upset, but decided that in our circumstances it was okay. My dad and I finally got food that was not even good, and we rode back to the hotel with some for my Mom.

After this disappointment, we were greeted to a filthy room and staff that didn't care. Sand and tissues covered the inside of our sheets. We were afraid to turn off the ceiling fan due to the three-inch layer of dust on top, and our shower curtain was slick with mold. The next ferry didn't come for twenty four hours; we were stuck. Of course.

Artist: Susan Biebuyck, Watercolor, "Jersey Girls"

Many more horrid events took place during our time before we left Fire Island. That was okay, though, because we did not go home after Fire Island. We decided we needed a vacation from our worst vacation ever. We went to the Hamptons for three days, which was extremely overpriced, but we decided we deserved it after the hell we had been through. The atmosphere there was lavish and beautiful; we had the most pristine rooms and beds with the fluffiest pillows I had ever felt. We took day trips to the beach, and at night we ate out and shopped. It was glamorous and quite the opposite of Fire Island.

So, although Fire Island was beyond unpleasant, it was unforgettable and brought us closer together. We laugh about it now and tell the story when we or others think things are going badly on a trip. We learned never to go back there and never to take advice from those family friends again. We also learned to come up with our own vacations from that point forward.

I personally learned that I can always trust and rely on my mom and dad: even if they really screw something up, they will do anything in their power to make up for it. That is love. I actually look forward to our next bad vacation.

~*Edie Biebuyck*

Edie Biebuyck is a student at West Chester University. She prefers to write memoirs about her travels with her offbeat family. She is currently working on a children's book about the stories her mother invented to entertain her when she was small.

A Note to My Muse:

"I'll be your mirror
Reflect what you are, in case you don't know."
                    - The Velvet Underground

You are the best thing to happen
  to me
  to this family
  to the world

Love yourself and know who you are
  change what you hate
  celebrate what you love
  seriously, use what you've got

Understand, we are ALL vulnerable
  be compassionate for the weak
  KNOWLEDGE will protect you from ignorance
  be STRONG

Liberate yourself
  free of fear
  unconstrained
  explore the earth

Search for true love
  in your friends
  in your mate
  in the music
  in your job

LOVE can surround you
  Protect you
  hurt you and heal you

let you soar
Ours is forever.

It's all in your hands
  your heart
  your conscience
  your journey

FLY baby fly
  buzz
  soar
  procreate

I will forever be here
  watching
  waiting to hold you for bit
  and set you free again

~*Susan Biebuyck*

Nourishing her own creative spirit, Susan Biebuyck has been an artist all her life. She attended Kutztown University in Pennsylvania. She is known for her acrylic, oil, pastel and watercolor painting diversity. She calls herself "an art supplies junky." Her work demonstrates superb observation and lyrical spirit. She has won honors and awards for exceptional painting. She was an inaugural GoggleWorks studio artist in Reading, Pennsylvania. In 2008, she started Studio B in Boyertown, Pennsylvania, with Jane E. Stahl where she is the Gallery Director & Curator. At the printing of this book the two women and numerous volunteers have promoted over 90 exhibits and hundreds of artists.

Artist: Hector Zelidon, Photograph, "Cosmopolitan"

THE WORLD NEEDS OUR LIGHT

"Darkness cannot drive out darkness, only light can do that."
Dr. Martin Luther King, Jr.

In the past few years the world has lost an extraordinary number of musicians, artists, writers—creative spirits of all types. As each creative light, one after another, went out—Maya Angelou…David Bowie…Leonard Cohen—I sensed the world getting darker, as if a cloud were rolling in over the sun. I felt a growing sense of fear and urgency to push back against it.

The recent swell of anxiety-inducing vitriol, violence, and venom seems to me a testament to this encroaching darkness. Old prejudices have resurfaced. Fear, mistrust, and uncertainty run rampant. Darkness causes people to want to contract, to withdraw within safe boundaries, old patterns, old belief systems; but what is needed is the opposite.

It is precisely at times like these that the world needs creativity the most. Literature, art, music, creative thinking bring light to the world. Light brings warmth, and warmth causes expansion.

Inspired by Martin Luther King's words, I am studying to be a Creativity Coach to enhance my abilities to encourage, inspire, and teach others to tune up and turn up their creative light. I have a new sense of urgency to bring my dream to reality—creating a space where writers, visual artists and other creatives can work their magic.

We all have a creative spark within us. Some burn brightly, others are a flickering candle, while others have been reduced to smoldering embers. Now is the time to fan the flame. The world needs our poetry, our stories, our art, our music, and the light we manifest through them.

Bringing beauty and joy into the world through creativity is a way to turn up the light and push back the darkness. I believe everyone has a spark of creative imagination that can add to the light, even if only in our own small circle of influence. This is my driving force—to make the world a brighter place through my own creativity and by lighting the creative spark in others.

(Portions of this article were previously published in the October 2016 issue of Creativity Coaching Association newsletter.)

> A creative spirit dies
> The world's light dims

Ghosts march in the street
Black spiders bloom on playgrounds

Everyone yells
Yet no one hears

Night falls. Fear abounds.
We curl inward—a cat in front of the fire on a cold night.

From your pen escapes a spark
From your brush, a blaze

Imagination ignites your mind
A neighbor catches fire

Flames dance. Heat radiates.
We expand and unfurl—the cat basking in its glow.

~ *Patty Kline-Capaldo*

Patty Kline-Capaldo is a writer, teacher, and creativity coach. Her passion is supporting writers and visual artists in their creative endeavors. Patty hosts two Meetup groups, where writers and artists gather for instruction, mutual encouragement, and inspiration: Just Write (http://www.meetup.com/Just-Write-in-Collegeville-PA) and The Artist's Way Circle (http://www.meetup. com/The-Artists-Way-Circle-in-Collegeville-PA/). She has also taught writing classes at Chester County Night School. Two of her memoir pieces have been published in anthologies: "Legacy of a Childless Woman" in <u>Slants of Light, Stories and Poems From the Women's Writing Circle</u> and "My Father's Daughter" in <u>The Life Unexpected, A Collection of Stories and Poems</u>. Patty earned her BA degree in Journalism and History from Indiana University and teacher certification from Ursinus College. She lives in Pottstown, PA, with her husband, Rich, and their three cats—Sarah, Splash, and Snapple. Read Patty's blog at http://pattyklinecapaldo.com/blog/.

Artist: Jennifer Swoyer, Acrylic on canvas, "Dark and Stormy"

Mentor for Glenna Holloway

Glenna could write like
the wind and sea
the earth and stone
the stars and sun

Glenna's work flowed
with the seamlessness
of an ocean tide
or toboggan run

Glenna could stun with
a sober verse
a soaring line
a single word

Glenna's rhymes rang
like the pleasing chime

of a silver bell
or a spritely bird

Glenna would prompt with
a cheerful voice
a thoughtful nod
a gentle sigh

Glenna's support
made my spirit sing
my efforts sail
my poems fly

~Carole Ziegler Croll

Carole Ziegler Croll was born in Pottstown, grew up in Schwenksville, and graduated West Chester University with a B.S. in Education. She began her career as a first grade teacher at Collegeville-Trappe Elementary School in 1973. After a move to the Chicago area, she became a licensed massage therapist, as well as a teacher of English Language Learners in the Wheaton School District. Her book, The Gift Forthcoming, is a collection of poems about love, beauty and spirit. Carole's work has appeared in various publications, and has been awarded by the Nevada Poetry Society, Poets and Patrons of Chicago, and the Illinois State Poetry Society.

Artist: Jonie Peters, Oil on canvas, "Embraceable Ewe"

EASY COME, EASY GO

Downstairs at the kitchen table
my parents played gin rummy
betting quarters and dimes

their voices overheard upstairs
muted but without argument
fans pulling unbridled air.

My parents happy.
Me in my room dancing with
my foldout poster of Bobby Sherman.

Nothing in this world I couldn't do.

I was in love
chasing rainbows in my mind

the world's suffering remote,
a distant land I'd read about in library books,
no worries about what I could remember

or what might be forgotten.
It was four years
before nuclear meltdown.

Back then corn stalks
unfurled like flags
in easy come, easy go fields.

~ *Sandra Fees*

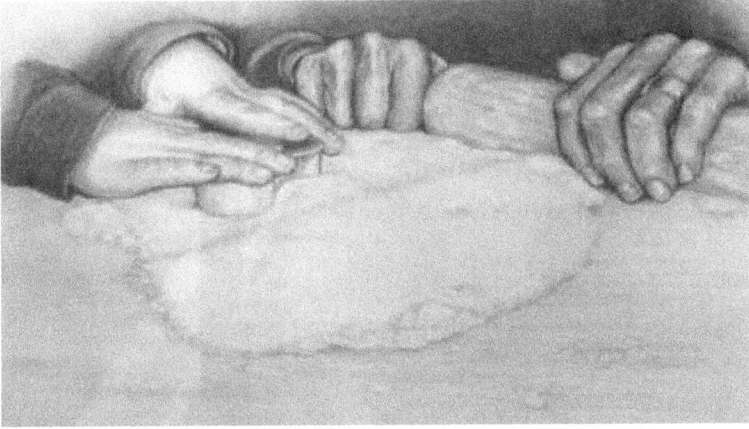

Artist: Tammy Updegrove, Charcoal/soft pencil, "A Day with Grandma"

FOOD FOR THOUGHT

It's Thanksgiving 2016.
Crossing the red bridge

inverted on water,
I recall a 1000-piece

jigsaw puzzle titled
Autumn Covered Bridge

assembled as my father
watched the evening news

warning the TV and me:
that man is a liar

meaning Richard Nixon.
At 15, I wondered how he knew

before the rest of us.
Now, feeling the demand

to sort truth from fiction
I miss his terse advice

he dubbed food for thought
and prefaced with the word dear.

Dear, keep a stiff upper lip
meaning history swings back

if you help it. Here's how he knew:
he found something to love

stayed where he was
worked his hands.

~ *Sandra Fees*

Sandra Fees is a Unitarian Universalist minister, residing in Reading, Pennsylvania. Her poems have been published in numerous journals, and her poetry chapbook, The Temporary Vase of Hands, is forthcoming from Finishing Line Press in February 2017. She has been named Berks County Poet Laureate for 2016-18.

Artist: Jesse Moore, Oil, "Crossway"

ROOSTING

"Therefore, all we really have to guide us is the response of joy and reverence we feel in the presence of what seems to us beautiful, good, and holy." From The Love of Impermanent Things *by Mary Rose O'Reilley*

Two days after the sugar maples are tapped, the aconite and snow drops rock the moist dirt, and the air smells like spring, feels thinner—not so heavy, repressive, hard.

It's past sunset, but the sky blues yet. The puppy plays Frisbee with me, and then stops at the sound of a crack in the treetops. He shows me the direction, and after the second thwap, I see it: a turkey—unwieldy, discombobulated—roosts in a tree at the wood's edge. Once stilled I lose sight of the bird, but another, and then another and then more ascend into the trees, three and four and five at a time. Flopping, loud, inelegant in every way, and it is gorgeous, these bumbling fools. I count twenty-one, but I know there are twenty-seven in the flock. The turkeys have been flaunting themselves, and we've been swapping stories with the neighbors about them.

Minutes pass, and the birds readjust infrequently now. I catch just a glimpse of a snood hanging inches below a beak or an outstretched wing silhouetted against the gloaming. The pup has turned to chew on a log, every once in a while nudging my calf, reminding me we're here, this is real. Then the six o'clock church bells go, and I look in their direction, and through the naked trees, I can see the bell tower, its warm little glow on the next ridge two miles away.

I'm not religious, but I think of my father-in-law, the brain tumor remnants they're killing with chemicals and lasers. I'm not comfortable with prayer. I'm too insignificant in these galaxies and eons, dinosaurs, and Sanskrit—too giant in this world of atoms, moss, a single grain of creek bed sand. All I know how to do: please, I ask. I try not to beg or whine.

And then the turkeys creak the branches again. When they finally settle, it's silent, and I would never know they were roosting, couldn't pick out their silhouettes, their beards or wattles or caruncles. I just have to trust, to know: they are there. Waiting till morning to descend in cacophonous, ungraceful bundles. Winging to the ground until again they alight to the sky.

~ Heather E. Goodman

Heather E. Goodman lives in a log cabin by a creek with her husband Paul and works as a private tutor and editor. Her fiction has been published in Gray's Sporting Journal, Shenandoah, Hunger Mountain, Crab Orchard Review, and the Chicago Tribune, where her story "His Dog" won the Nelson Algren Award. Visit her at www.heatheregoodman.com.

artist: jennifer hetrick, photograph, "river"

BARBARA TUCKER TAKES TO WATER
WHEN SHE WRITES WHIMS OF POETRY

you write like water, like the river,
barbara. it is something beautiful
to notice, to take in, whatever waves

are when they're less broad, moving
their route southeast but free of salt
like what sloshes around in the sea.

your language pours outward with
this natural flow so fitting that it is
a little hard to fathom—graceful

and deep like the caverns and all
complexity in your heart. it doesn't
surprise me that you live less than

six miles from a river, the schuylkill,
and that its name means *hidden river*
in dutch from the explorers who

aimed ships here around 400 years
ago (its previous name from the native
americans was turtle river, or tool-pay

hanna and also *turtle place or tool-pay
hok ung*). none of this surprises me, but
the better water in your inching words

always tugs behind my ribcage ever
so slightly in a way which teaches me

that i love land, wet sections around

    it, and students who embrace this all.

        ~ jennifer hetrick

artist: jennifer hetrick, photograph, "under the cherry tree"
artist of boyertown's bear fever bear, arline christ

JUST UNDER THE CHERRY TREES
FOR ARLINE CHRIST

red bear of sky
        stands below
                the orchard,

    painted feet
            planted in grass.

    its mother is of feathers, her quiet wisdom
housed at the end of mitch road in lower pottsgrove.

    ice-hued and night-colored trees

reach across the bear's back,

listening to the butter sun speak,

sing light,   lyricize heat.
that red holds our knees, taps our clavicles,   forgives   us
while teaching us lessons about the brightest warmth we

can't see.   it is in our   bones,   behind our eyes,

in the sudden, unanticipated twitch of a toe, a pinprick

in a shoulder blade's meat when we are carrying nothing—
but really, everything—of the world just below

our necks.

red bear. is. a. reminder. a story.

hard, beautiful magic. more.

~ *jennifer hetrick*

Jennifer Hetrick considers herself a language thrower of sorts. Through grants from the Pennsylvania Council on the Arts and Berks Arts Council, Hetrick manages a three-year project called the labors of our fingertips: poems from manufacturing history in berks county. Visiting schools and state parks to practice poetry with kids, she also teaches flash fiction as well as a traveling poetry class which often meets by the Schuylkill River. And she loves the sky.

Artist: Susan Biebuyck, Acrylic, "It's You, No, It's You"

FOR THE CHILD

she is six

silent

hidden

darkness

tears

face hidden

no words

waiting

waiting

waiting

hidden

within

she is 56

vocal

open

light

smile

face seen

words

speaking

speaking

speaking

open

for

the

Child

~Pamela Hodges

Pamela Hodges paints, writes, and cleans seven litter boxes. She is the typist for her cat who wrote the book, "How to Be a Cat." She lives in PA with one husband, three children, six cats, and two dogs. She writes about art, creativity, and everyday life on her website, ipaintiwrite.com. She is also the typist for her cat who blogs at TheCatWhoWrites.com

MINDFULNESS

I am energy

Constant

Flowing

Like a swift and steady river

I feel it

The power

Within

and around me

The merging of soul

Spirit

And

Substance

A cosmic

Vibration

Moving between

Muse

Sounds and silence

I am

Perception of life

Personal and absolute

~ L.T. James

Artist: Susan Biebuyck, Oil, "Pagoda View -en plein air"

POETS

Who are these people

We read

Love and loathe

From eons ago

Nash

Novalis

Paz and Wilde

Emerson and Hughes

Will they

Forever be cherished

By the present

Not just then

But how

What will happen to us

    As we

        Live

           Love

              Write

Slipping away into obscurity

    If no one reads

Forevermore

~ *L.T. James*

L.T. James has traveled around the world mostly on her own by sea, land, air, and on foot working, writing, photographing, and getting to know people of all different cultures and beliefs. Her work as Command Liaison for the Navy and Marine Corps led her to Japan for a three-year tour of duty where she also taught English and stayed in a monastery.

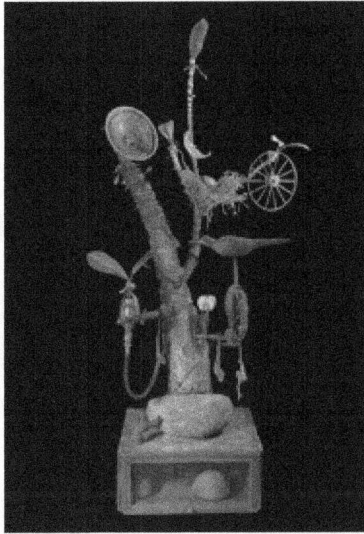

Artist: Bob Hakun, Sculpture, "Music of the Stones"

PURPOSE

All of my life I have repurposed words,
Ripped nouns apart
Turned them inside out,
Re-sewn them into serviceable verbs
That I now wear to a critique group,
Where we writers
Lead each other out of blindness
With a ritual of call
For new work and a,
"Thanks for the feedback."

The writer's job is to lead
Pied piper style,
Ask the millipede
What it's like to march…
Ask the horse
What it's like to horse around…

Lunacies and fantasies
That heave the tire out
Out of the rutted track
Of logical thought.
This is not an easy task,
Even if our readers
Are volunteers.
Some engineer
Among us will
Half rise from his chair
And point out
The fallacy of thus and so…
Lemon seeds slipping out of acid flesh
But my springboards are
So mundane, they barely
Count for anything:
A loose door knob
A tire with a slow leak
A dripping faucet
Rattling window panes
A curl of peeling paint
The speed of rust
A bent penny
The hubris of a house built on a river bank
A sagging barn door

What inspires me to write?
You do.

Marilyn L.T. Klimcho

Marilyn L.T. Klimcho is the Treasurer of Berks Bards, Inc., a grassroots poetry group centered in Reading. In addition to writing poetry, she also writes short stories and has recently tackled writing a screenplay. Her work in short story was nominated for a Pushcart Prize by the <u>Schuylkill Valley Journal</u>.

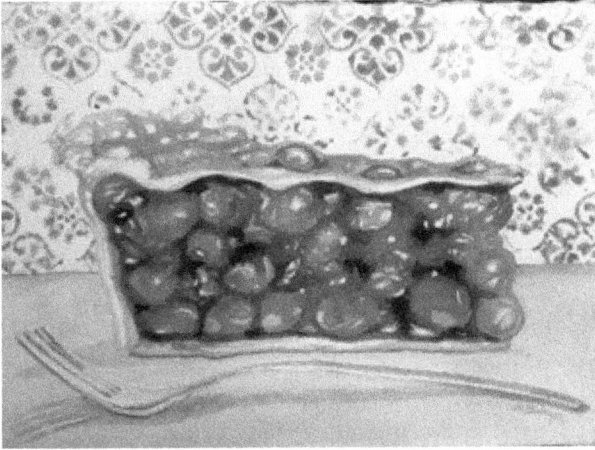

Artist: Susan Biebuyck, Watercolor, "Piece of Pie"

SHARING

The old man sitting in a booth with his wife

steadies his shaky hands to cut a piece of cheesecake in half.

He studies it like a diamond cutter ready to cleave a precious gem.

Tension in his face, holding the plate with his left hand,

he makes the perfect equal cut from the front point to the back.

Using the extra plate the waitress brought, he serves his wife.

Slowly unrolling the napkin, she places the knife, fork, and spoon,

tucks the white starched napkin under her chin,

and reaches across to the middle of the table

where their eyes and hands meet.

~ Ollie Koehler

THE OLD BOX CAMERA

A Kodak the size and shape

Of a box of Kleenex

Wrapped in grained black leather

With genuine leather handle.

Remembering all the yesterdays

The good times

The picnics in the grove at Hershey Park

The new car

Easter Sundays after church.

Each its own moment in time

Have all blown away

Leaving a shell

This box of Kleenex

With all the tissues gone.

~ *Ollie Koehler*

Ollie Koehler is enjoying the eighth decade of his life. He began his writing career at age 78 and is already a prize-winning poet. Last year he won first prize in the Berks Encore Senior Poetry Contest.

Artist: Joe Hoover, Watercolor, "Winter"

SEASONAL HYPNOSIS

"Now, begin counting backwards from 10 to 1 and just relax."
The stench of depression and anxiety permeates from the leather couch
I am lying on.
The temperature in the room quickly plummets and it turns to Winter.
We cannot find a pulse!
Men and women in blue uniforms scramble,
As I pick at my cuticles until they bleed.
Neighbors gather like vultures that can smell impending death.
Sirens pierce my eardrums and I press my hands over my ears.
I just stare down at the tips of my dirty Converse high tops.
We are losing her!
I wrap my frigid arms around my knees and sway back and forth.
Snowflakes fall silently and blanket the hysteria in my driveway.

The swirling red lights reflecting off the sidewalk make my head spin.
I hear fingers snap and my skin begins to thaw.
I stare in confusion at the mahogany ceiling tiles and the snow is melted.
I walk out of the office with a bottle filled with tiny white pills,
And a promise that I will only be able to recall, Spring, Summer, and Fall.

~*Catherine Mahony*

Catherine Mahony, a writer in multiple genres, studied professional writing at Kutztown University. She holds Associate in Arts degrees in Communications and Liberal Arts from Reading Area Community College, where she received the Creative Writing Award for academic excellence. Mahony earned two awards from the Community College Humanities Association for pieces that appeared in Legacy, RACC's literary journal, and was a finalist in the 2014 Norman Mailer High School and College Awards Competition in the category of Creative Nonfiction. She has been published in Front Street Journal, Nota Bene, Agony and Ecstasy: Reflections Inspired by Our Lives, Layers of Language: Idioms and Favorite Expressions, To Be: Know Thyself...You Do You, Rag Queen Periodical, and Lehigh Valley Vanguard. Cat's published works include her first chapbook of poetry entitled "Prior Restraints," which contains compelling images by photographer, Tamie Dickson, depicting her lifetime struggles with addiction and mental illness and In Knots: Motherhood Lost and Found, a collection of poetry and prose accompanied by photography by Andy Schön and fine artist Laura Gelsomini, that offers raw insights into a lifetime of loss, recovery, resilience, and hope.

BLESSINGS

I was introduced to poetry and the band Nine Inch Nails at around the same time. I loved both right away. Trent Reznor's unique sound stood out from all of the other artists I'd ever heard. I played around with writing poetry for a few years and had fun reading it.

It wasn't until after I was sexually assaulted and later raped that I put these two inspirations together. I would listen to the music while I scrubbed away my pain and sorrow. I'd keep it playing while I cried myself to sleep. His words spoke to me and I felt a release when it would echo in my mind.

Soon, I would begin writing the lyrics out. It felt so therapeutic to write that I decided to put my own words down on paper. I promised myself from that point on that I would write when I was feeling down. Instead of drowning in my own despair, I would release it.

To this day, the same music rings new struggles and conflicts in my heart. I listen to him to inspire my own art. He changed the way I deal with my heartache and may have saved my life. The below lyrics are an example of the many dark words that spoke to me when I was in such a wretched place in my own life.

The Only Time
~ Trent Reznor of Nine Inch Nails

I swear. I just found everything I need.
The sweat in your eyes, the blood in your veins are listening to me.
Well, I want to wrap it up and swim in it until I drown
my moral standing is lying down.
Nothing quite like the feel of something new.

I would use my new-found hobby to keep me from going off the deep end. I wrote a poem entitled "I Awoke to Die" about the time I was raped. Even though I wrote this poem years after the fact, it shows how long it can take to cope with pain. Some wounds will never heal, but finding a way to get through it and to express it helps to ease.

I Awoke to Die

He put me in a room
While I was asleep
He would secretly consume
All that he could reap

While I was asleep
He thought he could win
All that he could reap
As he sweat on my skin

He thought he could win
All I could do was cry
As he sweat on my skin
And I awoke to die

All I could do was cry
When he put me in a room
And I awoke to die
As he would secretly consume.

The next two poems I wrote about the music of Nine Inch Nails showing how deeply you can feel words, how words can impact your thoughts, decisions and feelings about yourself and those around you and about love, and life.

The third poem is about inspiration in all its forms. I would hope that the reader would take something away from my poetry, but that's not why I write. I write for me. I listen to music for me. I share my words because if Trent Reznor never shared his, I may never have written mine.

NOTHING CAN STOP ME NOW

Your guiding role in this
cruel, unforgiving life is
crucial liquidation for the
fire inside. It proves the only
reminder for which time
cannot revive. Your explanation I
can see, and your deep soul really
makes mine try. Keep making me feel
low enough so I might feel alive.

This is a "golden shovel" poem. The same song I mentioned earlier. "Nothing can stop me now" is repeated many times throughout multiple albums by Nine Inch Nails.

EVERYTHING IN YOU

Please, throw me into your pool
Deep within worlds beyond here
So warm, and brutally cool
Where I will drown away fear
The awakened moments shine
Piercing death into the ground
Exposing what's truly mine
And all that I haven't found
As I listen to the walls
Echoing the sound of you
Walk through, expecting to fall
I lose what I aim to do
But find a small piece of me
That I desperately forgot
So that I could really see
Everything that I am not.

Artist: Marianne Cerra, Photograph, "The Imprisoned Soul"

APPRECIATING INSPIRATION

Intensity increases in my
Inevitable inspiration of injustice
Recovering from rejection of the reprise
of my repetition in bliss
Expanding my extraordinary angst
Excelling in exploratory rapture
Throwing thoughts of thanks
Through thoughtless doors
Though my mind may minimize
Merely moping around
Asking mercy amid his eyes
Allows ambiguous abundant sound.

~ *Heather McArthur*

Heather McArthur is a wife and mother of three extraordinary children who has lived and worked in the Boyertown area her entire life. Someday she hopes to own a house and write a book for her children to pass along to their children. Heather feels blessed to have everything she needs or wants in her family and community.

A LEGACY

It didn't take long for Charles "Doc" McKinney to show appreciation for a saying that resonated well with him and his values. "Doc" was my grandfather and passed a decade before I was a blimp on the radar screen of my parents.

It was said that he only went to the third reader. Though you sure couldn't tell as his ability to figure things out meant that he lived up to his nickname. People hovered around him to ask for advice with some project or situation that they got themselves into. We folks have always created issues for ourselves. His was a "listening" persona and that became a positive glitch that got coiled up in my own DNA strands.

I could tell that he left his mark on my dad and on my aunt and on my uncle. "Gram" was his wife, and she was his "quiet" to his even quieter self, it was said. Doc's mind was always thinking and enjoyed being nourished by words and sayings. His saying that he really appreciated resonates with me still from my "young lad" days.

It goes like this: *"There is always some good in the worst of us and always some bad in the best of us, that it hardly behooves any of us to talk about the rest of us."* He helped me understand that our definitions of bad and good are left to our own devices. (Although it is taken as a given that we are not talking about mass murder or anything like that at all.)

Doc's saying was painted on a small plank of solid wood like the man that he was. It still hangs in the homestead's back porch to showcase its meaning to any visitor.

Doc left his legacy and was a talented woodworker and carpenter, thus inspiring my dad to pursue chores that other dads would not do. This example motivates me to go that extra step, and that is always a good challenge.

~*Patrick McKinney*

Patrick McKinney hails from Marion, Ohio, and now resides in Saint Clair, PA. He graduated from Ohio State with a degree in Environmental Interpretation and has worked for many years as education coordinator for the Schuylkill Conservation District. Known as "Porcupine Pat" he enjoys doing programs for people of all ages and sharing the wonders of nature through hikes and other outdoor-oriented opportunities. His hobbies include: biking, hiking, nature photography, drawing and painting art, and chilling with friends and family.

ONE

I met Flossie, my first yoga teacher, in 2003. The United States was getting ready to invade Iraq for the second time. Politicians were telling us that Saddam Hussein was making weapons of mass destruction and the State Department claimed to have proof. I didn't know whether the evidence was valid or fabricated. I didn't know whether the war was avoidable or necessary. But none of that mattered much because, either way, I felt helpless to stop it.

It was during this dark period that a friend was launching her career as a life coach. She organized a mini-retreat in the Pine Barrens of New Jersey that included a yoga class, and I wanted to support her. I also hoped that some time in Nature would take my mind away from worldly troubles and lift my spirit, so I signed up to participate.

The yoga class was held outdoors in the all-healing sunshine. I found it remarkable that holding a standing pose known as "Warrior" could create a state of serenity. Keeping my body active, yet motionless, forced me to stay in the present moment, and in that moment there were no worries. I felt gratitude for the strength in my thighs, calves, feet, and shoulders. I listened to Flossie's reminders not to strain, not to resist what is, to honor the limits of my body. If we couldn't achieve the pose physically, she said, we could visualize it, because the brain couldn't tell the difference.

Near the end of the class, we settled into the resting pose called *savasana*. Lying on my back, feeling relaxed and receptive, I heard Flossie say the words that changed how I see my life and its influence on planet Earth: "I know that many of us are feeling distressed about the impending war in Iraq. And maybe there is a feeling of helplessness.

But you are here, doing yoga. *And what you do for yourself, you do for the world."*

I felt a massive weight dislodge from my chest, rise up, and disappear.

A mathematician by nature, I tend to look for the logic behind the belief. I like to have proof. But on that day, I felt the truth of those words in every molecule of my being, as if remembering some long-forgotten wisdom that I'd brought with me when my soul entered physical form. To quote a more famous mathematician, Blaise Pascal, "we know the truth, not only by the reason, but also by the heart."

Thirteen years later, we still see a culture of fear, power, and separation. But behind the scenes, I see acts of kindness, love, and generosity that are rarely covered by the news media. I am only one person, doing what I can to raise my vibration—with yoga, prayer, and meditation. Only one person, spending time in Nature, listening to happy music, viewing beautiful art, contributing my own joy to the collective consciousness. As transcendental meditation founder Maharishi Mahesh Yogi described it, "a positive change in one individual is good enough to radiate its influence, just as a small lighted filament is enough to light a whole room."

What we think about matters. What we do for ourselves matters. Because we are all connected. Together, we are the critical mass that creates our world.

~ By Virginia McNamara

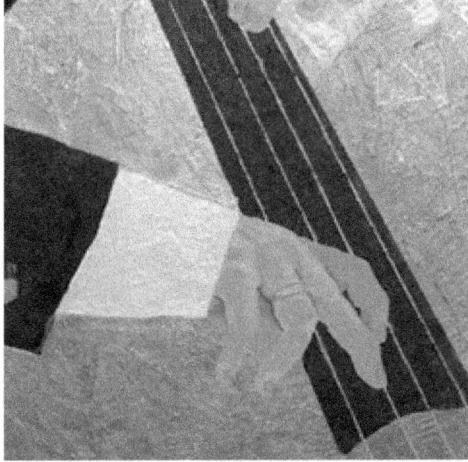

Lynn Millar, Acrylic, "Strings"

APPLAUSE FOR THE MILKY WAY

For experiencing Nature at her most inspiring, it's hard to go wrong with Ontario's Bruce Peninsula National Park. The tropical colored water of the Georgian Bay and the chiseled cliffs of the coastline are mood altering. The forces of Nature that transform the landscape are also transforming me, polishing away the dark outer layers, revealing what is bright and beautiful inside.

I'd chosen this destination because I was starving for silence. An online search about the park made a reference to "dark sky," and I knew that if a place is dark enough to see stars, it probably is quiet, too.

In the suburbs of Philadelphia, even late at night, I cannot find silence. The relentless hum from the refrigerator and the elevator's hydraulic system affect me even during sleep, bothering the part of my brain that handles guard duty without actually waking me. What does wake me is the nearby freight train. The concrete building magnifies the sound of the train's horn—creating the illusion that the train has derailed and is heading directly toward my bedroom window.

Unable to sleep after a train episode, I'd started to think about the
upcoming trip and the stars that I so rarely get to see. Then I thought
about the moon and the fact that men had walked on her surface in my
lifetime while my ancestors were convinced that the earth was flat. I
wondered what humanity's next big epiphany might be…perhaps the
revelation that we all emanate from the same source, with the same
right to life, liberty, and happiness. The weightiness of that thought
had been exhausting enough to send me back to sleep.

When my husband and I arrived in Canada, we stayed in the small
town of Tobermory, Ontario, and hiked the nearby trails in the
national park. On our third night there, when the sky was clear and
the moon nowhere in sight, we drove several miles south of town to
the Singing Sands nature center. Light pollution was low enough that
we needed a flashlight to find the boardwalk into the marsh area. We
killed the light, felt our way along the boardwalk for 30 or 40 yards,
then stopped to look up. Clusters of stars, some nearer than others,
some densely packed and some spaced apart, formed a luminous
band that stretched from horizon to horizon, hinting at the depth of
the universe. Only centimeters above the earth, thousands of insects
were making a sound like the whir of miniature helicopter blades. The
sound fluctuated in volume as it came in waves from every direction.

I hadn't found the total silence I'd been looking for, but this was better.
The show was in the sky above, and the applause for it was swirling
around my feet. Standing in the middle of the marsh, I felt the same
kind of excitement that I'd felt at the Academy of Music in Philadel-
phia, when Daniel Barenboim played four of Beethoven's piano sona-
tas. At the end of the first sonata, the applause was tremendous and
long lasting. When it died down, Daniel said something like this: "I
noticed that one enthusiastic member of the audience applauded in the
space between the first and second movements and that he was imme-
diately shushed by the people around him." The audience chuckled,
and Daniel continued. "When you are moved by something, when you

are filled with awe and you feel like you want to applaud, you should do it!"

Standing in the starlight, I wondered if I could merge my appreciation onto the sound waves of the insects' song, and, if I did, could it reach the Milky Way. But then I decided that my thoughts are waves of energy, gratitude is energy, and who is to say how far that energy travels?

The Milky Way experience, the Beethoven sonatas, and the kind words of the man who performed them still inspire me. When I look for it, I see a thread that connects all of these things. Why does pressing piano keys in a certain sequence, with a certain intensity and timing, take the listener out of a mundane way of being, dissolve doubts and worries, and replace all of that with bliss? Why did the words of Daniel Barenboim, in his homage to the passionate expression of awe and gratitude, bring a lump to my throat? I believe that something embedded in the music, in the performance of that music, in Daniel's gesture and in his message, is the same something that radiates from the stars, a light that we respond to because we have a spark of it inside of us. That spark is sometimes dimmed under the weight of the world, patiently waiting to be reignited by Nature's power, divinely inspired music, a kind word, or starlight from the Milky Way that travels for thousands of years to reach us on a dark, moonless night.

~ *Virginia McNamara*

Virginia McNamara is retired from the field of mathematics, telecommunications, computer software development, and technical writing. Currently she creates oil paintings, poems, and essays that are inspired by travel experiences or life lessons. A memoir about working in Moscow, Russia, is currently in progress.

artist: **jennifer hetrick,** *photograph, "plains coreopsis"*

A Touch of Heaven

A break in the sidewalk reveals a precious gift.
A delicate, colorful flower so skillfully and beautifully designed.
Who created this stunning marvel?
For what purpose?
Why here? Why now?

Will anyone stop to discover and ponder
The exceptional care and love that fashioned it?
Perhaps a freckle-faced child strolling aimlessly down the sidewalk
Or an old woman stooped over from a lifetime of toil
Will pause, examine, and appreciate the intricate handiwork.

Alas, many are far too busy.
Too distracted.

Too self-absorbed
To notice the gift and wonder about the giver.

Daily the creator provides touches of His glory as free gifts
Sometimes in the most unusual places or unlikely people.
Hints of His existence and creativity scattered throughout the universe.
Compelling little bits of evidence of a rich, delightful, now hidden afterlife

For all who choose to believe.

~ *Patricia Petrowicz*

Pat Petrowicz is a wife, mother, and former junior high social studies teacher. In retirement she tries to keep fit by participating in an exercise class 2 or 3 times a week and by walking in her neighborhood. To keep her mind from turning to mush, she has become addicted to solving crossword puzzles and Sudoku, and to reading extensively about religion and politics. She spends a significant amount of time involved with her church, where she serves as a lector, altar server, and choir member.

Susan Biebuyck, Photograph, "Newcastle Street Beach"

DUST AND DEW

I am both the dust and dew
That rides upon the wind
And I cannot tarry here too long,
For in the swells of sand and time
My time is but a song –
The song, which heard, passes by into yesterday.
And so it is with dust and dew
That rides upon the spray.

~*P.A. Pizzi*

YOU PITY ME

You pity me
For I have lost the lover's sweet illusion
And walk alone through green meadows
And freshly fallen snow,
And wonder why
You pity me.
But it is I who pity you –
For when my heart does sing its love song to my mind,
I once again shall walk the green meadows –
And dance upon the snow.
Now it is I who pity you.

~P.A. Pizzi

P.A. Pizzi lives a quiet life in the country and is a sculptor and a writer.

Jillian Wright Prout, Watercolor, "Dream Tree"

MARGINS

"Hurry up. You're slowing me down. Pay attention. You're drifting; how will you ever keep up," they keep demanding.

My little legs just can't keep up. Seems to be my lot in life. Born small, grow slow; everyone is taller and faster. Moving, singing, hearing the beat of my own drum, never really fitting in and always the new girl.

Learning to follow my own senses and not bothering with what others thought, I slowed further, looked inward for directions. Being an observer allows a knowing, a seeing, and an acceptance of variety in all.

In order to flee from the pushing and pulling of the ubiquitous needs and impossible expectations of others, the wild, slow-growing trees drew me to their stalwart sides and shady floors. Sitting next to a rough trunk, looking up through the stainless glowing bright leaves to the deep cerulean blue sky, serenity settles, creativity bubbles.

Thoughts waft like cloud shadows across the gently rolling landscape. Viewing ideas as if watching the reflections of birds soaring overhead like boats upside down floating by off the big silvery lake reposing against the dark green mountain. Resting on a moss-covered, needle-strewn floor, all anxiety, all the demanding voices, drain away.

Winds blow stirring thoughts; leaves rustle; thoughts shift, and a quiet settles. A flashing of light, a realization, a sun rising, an illumination passes through, glowing with a new idea or project.

Bold, handwritten black letters tell the story, impart the knowledge, express the thoughts. Inky scratchings on a surface, trying desperately to describe the abstract seem to fall short frequently. Add an image, and full illumination occurs.

Fractur, simple pictures to bring the dark stark written word into the light, fracturing a hard crisp concept into soft colorful cognition. Illuminated manuscript on dense skin page filled with carefully laid down descriptors made bright and attractive with pleasing pictures and valuable gold along the borders, holding the whole book together. Lying close to the threads that bind the leaves of a volume lovingly made.

Words fall short, as short as I, never able to fly off the fluttering leaves. The sun shines through the window onto the goldleaf-covered images, sees itself reflected back as understanding springs to life.

As the fresh red sunrise reaches each tendril across a sleepy lawn lighting each blade tip of grass lighting up every new green leaf hanging from the wild wood, so does the mind blaze up with the wild fire of understanding. So the quiet places, the wild places, the little known hideaways, the overlooked, the undervalued, the margins are where the magic is.

~ *Jillian Wright Prout*

Jillian Wright Prout, Watercolor & india ink, "Diurnal Nocturnal"

Slow Life

*Two wheels glide over the pavement, legs pumping straining to catch up—
again. Ladies' voices carry on the wind. Joining them, I lift my hands off the
bars. Hair flutters behind, gravity pulls perfectly downhill, arms out—balanc-
ing on my quietly humming bike.*

"Look, Ma, no hands."

O! So free! I know how to fly! The blue sky opens its arms and my soul soars.

Settling back down, gliding downhill, flowers smile up into the sun-
shine. Wildflowers of periwinkle—blue cornflowers, lemony yellow
mustard dandelion, and tiny white daisies scatter along the side of the
road, squeezed between the public-owned macadam and private prop-
erties of manicured lawns and useful fields.

The lawless edge, untamed by man, called useless, called weeds, yet
they persevere—uncultivated and savage. Even in the face of those with
superior intellect, big machines, mean poisons, and good intentions
are unable to domesticate them, conquer them. They thrive in their
own beauty and wildness on the edges. Flourishing, catching the eye
of those that slow long enough to see, to really see—not to pick, not to
own, but to love.

~ *Jillian Wright Prout*

*Due to my dyslexia, I came to writing late in life. I kept a journal of thoughts
but only started "putting it out there" when I joined Facebook. I am a wife, a
mother, a farmer, an artist, a yogini and now a writer. My education includes
a fine arts degree from Kutztown University, and 500 hours of yoga training,
plus a year at DePaul University for acting. My family moved a lot, but Lake
Dunmore, Vermont, is where I called home until my husband and I bought a
beautiful farm in Oley, Pennsylvania.*

Jillian Wright Prout, Watercolor & india ink, "Squash Blossom"

BAUBLES FOR PRUDENCE

My good friend Prudence Mayweather planned for the best
But prepared for the worst if calamity came.
She addressed the small chance life would deal her a loss.
All the same, she expected to grab the brass ring.

When she tossed up a bright coin and calmly cried, "Heads!"
Every thing made her think that she was a winner.
If instead her half dollar sat squarely tails up,
Her inner voice laughed with some slight indignation.

See the cup isn't empty to Prudence, so wise.
Since her station in life, as she lives it, is full.
For besides, isn't life what you make of it? Then
Just be cool when your destiny throws you a curve.

My good friend Prudence Mayweather loved things that shone,
Brightness served as reminder to follow her light.
When her poem read unevenly, rather than moan,
She held tight to the certainty all would be right

It is human to reach for the brightest and best,
But be careful - sometimes mere reflection can blind.
Your good prudence may help you to weather the storms
And remind you to dance through the puddles you find.

~ Philip Repko

Phil Repko is a career educator in the PA public school system who has been writing for fun and no profit since he was a teenager. Phil lives with his wife Julie in Gilbertsville and is the father of three outstanding children, two of whom are also poets and writers. He vacillates between poetry and prose, as the spirit beckons, and is currently working sporadically on a novella and a memoir.

Jay Ressler, Digital collage, "Sovereign Pledge"

THE MARCH OF THE ASHES

Wizened and nine decades wise
Student of Martí and Maceo
And of The Moor too;
Gabo's* friend died
An old man's death.

Gold Medal winner
Of an Olympic event never sanctioned
"Assassination Attempt Survivor,"
With 638 wins.
Tainted milkshakes and poisoned cigars;
Bomb plots and sniper shots;
Lover's treachery and mobsters' plots;
CIA-masterpieces from afar
Foiled every one,
He suffered without a scar.
Hundreds danced in glee
In the sinking city by the sea
When his passing
Made history.
But multitudes mourned,
Freedom Caravaners by the throng,
Streamed from Plain and Mountain abode,
To proclaim "I am He" in a song.
Large in life was he,
Orator for peasants and working women
And laboring men too,
Leader in battle — el commandante,
Though hated by barons and capitalist lords;
By wretched and oppressed
The Old Man was adored.
His emblazened battle banner
"¡Si Se Puede!"
"Yes, we can! Yes, We Will!"
Heartened fighters at
Moncada and Alegria de Pio,
Sierra Maestra and Playa Giron,
In Angola and Cuito Caunavale,

In the war against illiteracy,
Also in the Special Period
That emerged from a bitter sea.

Likened to David challenging Goliath
For him Internationalism did prevail,
Troops to defend Angola
Doctors abroad wherever need bloomed,
(More than those of the WHO)
His strategic daring tipped the scale
Assuring Nelson's freedom and Apartheid's doom.
Revolutionary worker and peasant organizer
With Vladimir Illych he stormed the heavens
Without falling to Stalin's vials of poison
The Old Man died an Old Man's death
A spoiler of all the aggressions.
A reader and man of letters too
The Old Man scolded Gabo
That in the fictions he conjured
Real-world facts
Need be written true.
That is the story of how the commander-in-chief
Became the fact-checker-in-chief,
Even before a soldier's fatigues he did quit
To sport a blue and white leisure outfit
In service of the man who imagined a century of solitude
A general's labyrinth, and love when cholera throve.
Along the 500-mile march
Of the Old Man's ashes
Thousands showed their homage
And millions made a pledge.
The procession's final halt
Crowded under the shadow
Of the Titan of Bronze—
Martyr of Punta Brava to exalt.
Beside a thousand raised machetes
His brother, The President, made clear
The terms of the Will of the Bearded One:
There would be no statue or public place
On which the Old Man's name or frame would appear.

The lone monument would be
The will and pledge of the fighting people
To defend their sovereignty
And integrity against arrogant hostility,
Multiplied by imperialist voracity,
By Leviathan of the North.
The Old Man's ashes were fated
For a grotto quite small
Near the Mausoleum for Martí
In a crowded veterans' stall
Bearing only his Christian name
On a humble cement wall.
Before the cremated remains
Of Gabo's friend received their final rest
Maceo's vow and warning were summoned,
"Whoever attempts to conquer Cuba
will gain nothing but the dust of her blood-soaked soil
— if they do not perish in the struggle!"
'Tis the honor the Old Man's life possessed.

*Gabriel Garcia Marquez

~ Jay Ressler

A native of Berks County, Jay Ressler graduated from Oley High School and Albright College. Before moving back to the area in 2014 he was active in the art scene in Pittsburgh for a number of years. Although he is now a full-time artist, during much of his working life we was at different times an underground coal miner and steelworker and active in union affairs. Ressler has a history of activism including in the civil rights and anti-Vietnam war movements.

Artist: Martha Ressler, Fabric painting, "Rusty Musty Fusty

RUSTY MUSTY FUSTY

Yo! I like 'em rusty and musty

Old city factories all scruffy

And in the country so crusty

They were cars or trains, all them parts so fusty

Lying around -- almost art -- a little fuzzy

The sun makes you just

Lovely though scruffy

That's OK I'm not fussy

I'll take you thusly

Beauty all rusty.

~ *Martha Ressler*

Martha Ressler makes, teaches and tirelessly promotes art quilts, which are a creative visual work that is layered and stitched. Ressler was a painter who loved to sew, so she has found her medium. She moved from Pittsburgh to Berks County 3 years ago where she has found renewed inspiration.

Tammy Updegrove, Charcoal, "Just Like Daddy"

SWEATING TEARS

Four a.m. – a cul de sac deep in trees –
an old woman lies motionless,
hands pressed to her forehead.
She sweats tears.

The joints of her fingers ache.
She's been digging stones, throwing
them aside, kneeling to create
fertile space for things to grow.

Now, eyes closed, she sees
the evening news. Images.
Allepo. Helping hands remove
a small boy's dust-heavy shirt.

Arms raised, silent, he stares ahead,
eyes shadowed. Fragile ribs encase
a narrow chest. Outside, an old man
lifts stones, one by one, and hurls them

down the mound of rubble on which
he squats. With every heave, he sobs.
Suddenly, he shudders, kneels, and,
face in hands, weeps for growing things.

~ *Nancy Rosenberger*

Nancy Rosenberger taught English in public high schools and in universities for 35 years. Her students' ages have ranged from twelve to eighty-four. Now retired, she is teaching literature and critical/creative thinking courses at Widener's OLLI Institute where she also leads monthly discussions on the writing and reading of poetry. Nancy has received two National Endowment Grants and has been acknowledged for her teaching by the Governor of Pennsylvania.

Joe Hoover, Watercolor, "First Blanket"

THE WOKE: A CONVERSATION TOWARD RECOVERY AND DISCOVERY

I was running late, as usual, and amused, as usual, that the front row of seats in any group meetings I'd ever attended were always the ones least taken—left to those, like myself, who couldn't manage to get anywhere early.

But, I smiled meekly to the speaker in apology for my tardy entrance; and, as he continued his introductory remarks, I recognized words that had served as my own mission statement during my career as a teacher of literature and writing.

"'Many, many men have been just as troubled morally and spiritually as you are right now. Happily, some of them kept records of their troubles. You'll learn from them—if you want to. Just as someday, if you have something to offer, someone will learn something from you. It's a beautiful reciprocal arrangement. And it isn't education. It's history. It's poetry.'"

The speaker continued, "Let Salinger's words to Holden, that iconic adolescent cynic, serve as our guide. Our new discussion group— 'Discovering Your Inner Phoenix'—hopes to inspire all of us to share not just the stories of our struggles, but also the stories of our rebirths and solutions. These stories are the 'poetry' Mr. Antolini offers Holden, 'poetry' that celebrates our triumphs and from which others can learn.

"But, let's get to it. You're here because you're hurting. You've suffered a major loss of some sort. Maybe a death, maybe a relationship or job, maybe a belief in something, maybe a belief in yourself or in life itself.

"Whatever the specifics of your loss, you all share one thing: your world has been shaken to its core in some regard. Your world has gone grey, lost its luster, and, worse, you're finding it difficult to care about any of it. Taking 'arms against [your] sea of troubles' seems pointless. Escape, distractions—even imagining yourself 'not to be' in this world any longer continue to surface as best case scenarios.

"But it is through our sharing that you will be energized in realizing that you are not alone. You'll begin to 'know thyself,' explore why you do what you do, and how you will make life better for yourself. You'll discover what you want and what you don't want in your life, and you'll regain your sense of purpose, your desire to be true to the person you choose to be.

"And I guarantee you—or double your money back—that with that knowledge, hope in yourself and the joy in your life that you've lost will return.

"But first, let's take a moment to visit the refreshment table and maybe say 'hello' to someone in the group you already know or to introduce yourself to those folks seated next to you. We'll begin the meeting in 10 minutes."

With that, the speaker approached me—seated reluctantly "front and center"—and extended his hand. Embarrassed, I offered a weak apology for my tardiness, but he smiled, winked, and offered, "Hi, I'm JD. No worries. I'm usually late myself. I'm just glad you're here. "

"And I think I'm happy to be here," I said, "especially since you intend to focus on solutions, not catalogues of our assorted miseries, tepid affirmations or polite pablum aimed at massaging our hurt egos. Seeking solutions: 'There's the rub.'"

"So, how might you define your loss," JD queried.

"Ha! Where do I start? Life's been a bit of an 'unweeded garden' for me of late. People I've loved—friends, family, even those I hardly know or those who work for me and my family—have betrayed my trust and belief in them and in who I thought they were. I have no one left. No one. And top of that I feel really stupid," I explained.

"Stupid? Why stupid?" he asked.

"Well, I've always believed that folks were generally kind, generous, respectful of one another—sometimes misinformed or uninformed, but 'coachable,' at least. In a word, I have lost faith and hope for change. I find that our souls are irrevocably diseased and ruled by fear, and I don't know how to respond to a world—and people—I don't recognize.

"I have been pathologically naïve in believing we were evolving morally, you know, 'bending toward justice' as Dr. King wrote. I was certain that Lincoln's 'better angels of our nature' would prevail and ultimately defeat the unrelenting brutality of the world. Yet, I'm appalled by the hatred and prejudice that has been uncovered and spreading recently within our country and within my very own family and friendship circle. I mean, I can understand one 'rotten apple or two,' but I realize that the entire bushel is rotten.

"Like you said, I no longer care…about anything or anyone…I yearn that 'my too, too solid flesh would melt.' I'm thoroughly repulsed by the ignorance, misogyny, and bigotry that has surfaced. I'm willing to kick long-time friends and my own family to the curb, as it were. Heck, I'm ready for my own 'quietus' and that 'undiscovered country from whose bourn no traveler returns.'

"And I believe that any other response to them makes me one of them or worse. I hate having to choose between my loved ones and my integrity. I'm so disgusted and angry all the time. But mostly, I'm profoundly sad and I can't imagine a path back to joy and purpose."

"You DO have reasons for your disillusionment," JD offered. "That's a lot to process as a young person. But, just so you know, I've been in your shoes. Unlike you, most of my despair came from my own actions.

"I was repulsed by who I had become. Totally lost. My journey back hasn't been easy, but because I've been there…and survived, I know that recovery of health and happiness is possible. And I know that those of us who have journeyed to the edge can be of invaluable assistance to others. But it ain't easy, my friend. That is for sure.

"But, as they say, or, rather as Viktor Frankl has said, 'that which doesn't kill you makes you stronger….' And those who have a 'why to live can bear most any how.' We need to talk strength-building and the understanding that, whatever fortune or misfortune attends us, 'Readiness is all….There is a special Providence in the fall of a sparrow.' We're not in charge of anything but our own attitudes. As they say, 'Let be.'

"Before we do that, it's good to acknowledge the grief. Grief has many stages as you know. Being here tonight suggests you're past the first three stages: denial, bargaining, and anger. Depression, the fourth stage, often takes the longest.

"But there is an inevitable fifth stage: acceptance. If you hang around long enough and, I guess, recognize the stages as a process and do the necessary work on our perceptions, 'acceptance' happens. In any case, 'whether or not it is clear to you, no doubt the universe is unfolding as it should.'

"But I don't mean to deny your pain. There is much trickery in this world, many loud and aggressive people, much sham and drudgery, and many broken dreams. Many folks have found a 'solution' or two from their practice of habits outlined in 'The Desiderata.' Check it out."

With these words, JD moved to address a few others in the group. I watched him as he moved confidently back to the stage offering a smile, a shoulder hug, or handshake to those he passed on his way.

"OK, so whatcha got?" he asked. "What has inspired you? How have you, as stardust, found your way back to the garden?"

"Words have helped me," a young man offered. "An English teacher John Keating shared that 'No matter what anybody tells you, words and ideas can change the world.' I believed him. And the words that mattered to me came from a poem by Sara Teasdale titled 'Barter.'

"I don't want to recite the entire poem, but certain images resonated with me: 'Blue waves whitened on a cliff' took me to the stony coast of Rockport, Massachusetts. 'Music like a curve of gold' brought me Pachebel's Canon in D minor; 'Scent of pine trees in the rain,/Eyes that love you, arms that hold' capture my joy.

"And her 'solution' is to 'Spend all you have for loveliness and never count the cost.'"

"Off to the mall then?" JD asked.

"No, no, never fear; she wasn't telling me to max out my credit card. Her lovelies actually aren't for sale. Her message is that I shouldn't waste my entire existence 'getting and spending.' Nature's sights and sounds, smells, feelings, and thoughts are free if we are aware of their beauty.

"Beyond the enjoyment of nature, William Wordsworth also offers Nature as spiritual inspiration," the young man continued. "He recognized the 'anchor of [his] purest thoughts, the nurse/The guide, the guardian of [his]heart, and soul/Of all [his] moral being' in 'nature and the language of the sense.'

"He gained a purer mind, tranquil restoration, feelings of pleasure and was inspired to 'little, nameless, unremembered, acts of kindness and of love.' No small things to those who despair."

The young woman beside me raised her hand to be acknowledged. "And I love the sonnet 'i thank you god' by e e cummings. The symphony of sound in his poem and the images of 'leafy greenly spirits of trees and a true blue dream of sky' makes me think about how he let all of his senses awaken. All of us can be that awake and inspired."

"You mentioned John Keating, from Dead Poet's Society, offered another young man seated beside her. I loved that movie and the advice he offered those young men regarding the reason for language: Keating said, 'Language was invented for one reason, boys - to woo women.' I love that line and have made it a point to increase my vocabulary."

With that, the group laughed and JD nodded in agreement.

"A more powerful quote from that movie came from Walt Whitman," noted an older man from the back of the room. "It inspired me following my suicide attempt as I searched for a meaning for my life. Whitman wrote, 'O me! O life!...of the questions of these recurring; of the endless trains of the faithless... of cities filled with the foolish; what good amid these, O me, O life? Answer. That you are here — that life exists, and identity; that the powerful play goes on and you may contribute a verse. That the powerful play goes on and you may contribute a verse. What will your verse be?'

"I am in search of my verse, but his words helped me understand that we are all here for a reason."

"The words that meant the most to me came from a play full of hate and revenge, murder and betrayal. Shakespeare's Christmas special—

King Lear, offered a young woman seated next to him. "If you know the play, it's difficult to believe that he wrote it for the fortnight surrounding Christmas.

"But just like many of the contemporary Christmas stories, the ending is all about forgiveness and love. The king, now a broken man in prison with his beloved daughter whom he punished earlier in the play, is finally broke and finally happy.

"His words say it all for me: 'Come on, let's go to prison. The two of us together will sing like birds in a cage. We will be good to each other. When you ask for my blessing, I'll get down on my knees and ask you to forgive me. That's how we'll live—we'll pray, we'll sing, we'll tell old stories, we'll laugh at pretentious courtiers, we'll listen to nasty court gossip, we'll find out who's losing and who's winning, who's in and who's out. We'll think about the mysteries of the universe as if we were God's spies. In prison we'll outlast hordes of rulers that will come and go as their fortunes change.'

"Everything he worked for his entire life had been taken away; he made some terrible decisions, treated people abominably; but in his final moments, he 'gets it.' Love is what matters; it's the perfect Christmas story ending!"

"Excellent," offered JD. We have time for a few more. Bruce, how about you."

"I'm concerned with all the 'bigotry, racism, intolerance that will be difficult to quell' with our current leadership. 'Whether it's a rise in hate crimes, people feeling they have license to speak and behave in ways that previously were considered un-American and *are* un-American. My fears are that those things find a place in ordinary civil society.' I've had a wake up call and I'm really not sure how to respond. I'm pretty discouraged, actually."

"Understood," JD said. "Yet your music has inspired many. I am reminded of the Chinese curse: 'May you live in interesting times.' We have arrived. OK, Cameron, your turn."

"'To see the interconnected and unrelenting brutality of the world is all-consuming and terrifying.…Being in a rage almost all the time is neither healthy nor satisfying….In my passion, I have often neglected the fact that love and beauty are necessary too and indeed are the goal of this continual fight against oppression. I wish I could figure out how to find a balance….For now I take solace in the fact that, every once in awhile if I am very lucky, I can help someone else wake up too.'"

"I think I can help here," came a voice from the back that everyone recognized instantly. '[W]hat we want to do is maybe accelerate [young leaders'] presence on the scene, and that's where I can be helpful, shine a spotlight on all the great work that's being done and all the wonderful young Americans who will help lead the way in the future.'"

Everyone rose in applause before he spoke again. "Let me just say this. Here's the thing that I learned from Mother Teresa and Andy Rooney many years ago. Mother Teresa reminds us that 'We can do no great things, but we can do small things with great love.'

"Andy Rooney reminds us that words are small things, but the right words, at the right moment have power to inspire or degrade, heal or wound, champion or discourage. Words can transform our lives and the lives of others.

"He recalled a time he was working as a reporter for 'The Stars and Stripes in London in 1943 when the Germans were regularly bombing the city. It was bad and much of London was laid waste. At the time, the editor of a London newspaper talked about how the English had reacted to the bombing raids that destroyed so much of their city.

"The editor wrote, 'When the first raid hit London, neither the government nor the newspapers knew what the people who had been hit were thinking and how they would take it. That evening, putting out the newspaper, we decided to assume from what evidence we had that they had acted heroically, and the next morning we printed all the stories that came in to us of their bravery, their good humor and their uncomplaining patience.

"'Right then, the newspaper fixed the pattern of how people ought to behave in an air raid. Perhaps they would all have behaved that way anyway. But you know'—and here's the thing—'there is a good and bad in all of us and the right example [the right words in this case] at the right moment can make all the difference in the way men act.'"

"And so folks, we can change the world…one word at a time. Possibly you recall wielding your own power through words. With your well-chosen words, you became a supporting actor who gave someone else's life story a happy ending or the encouragement to 'carry on.'

"I, too, have been discouraged profoundly in recent months. But I am encouraged by words—by the words of those very people who have suffered a great loss. Their words carry my spirit from its depths to a place where I can breathe and live again.

"So, my solution just for tonight is to choose your words carefully to give spirit a.k.a. *inspiration* to those around you as they demonstrate or work for peace, for compassion, and for love of all living things.

Then, giving a nod and flashing his signature smile, he added, "And with that, my friends, as the story goes, 'a good night!'"

Applause erupted as he saluted those in the group in uniform and made his way to the door, shaking hands along the way.

"Shalom," JD saluted in return. "And thank you for your service, Mr. President; we will certainly miss your intelligent leadership.

"As for us," JD continued, "we will consider additional solutions next week. Meanwhile, as suggested by the comments tonight: 'In the beginning was the Word.' Let yours continue to encourage and support. And always, 'Strive to be happy.'"

~*Jane Stahl*

****

This piece was first inspired by a Facebook post from a very special former student who, herself discouraged from recent events, shared an article that put into words the discouragement she felt. "The perils of being woke AF"—Cameron Brewer, Blavity.com, December 28, 2016. She offers her own mission found in a fortune cookie message: **"Human Rights: Know Them, Demand Them. Defend Them.**

*Jane apologizes to the following quoted in part loosely in the piece:
<u>Hamlet</u> by William Shakespeare
<u>King Lear</u> by William Shakespeare
<u>Catcher in the Rye</u> by J.D. Salinger
<u>Man's Search for Meaning</u> by Viktor Frankl
"Woodstock" by Joni Mitchell
"Barter" by Sara Teasdale
"i thank you god" by e e Cummings
"Lines Written a Few Miles Above Tintern Abbey" by William Wordsworth
"The World Is Too Much With Us" by William Wordsworth
"The Desiderata" by Max Ehrman
"Leaves of Grass" by Walt Whitman
<u>Dead Poet's Society</u>, screenwriter Thom Schulman
"Terror Is Not the Word," Andy Rooney, Jewish World Review, August 22, 2002/ 14 Elul, 5762
'Twas the Night Before Christmas," Clement Clarke Moore
"The perils of being woke AF"—Cameron Brewer, Blavity.com, December 28, 2016.
Interview with Bruce Springsteen on Trump, Channel 4 News, https://youtu.be/1_UoZ8wP6zg
David Axelrod Interviews President Barack Obama for The Axe Files, December 26, 2016, http://www.cnn.com/2016/12/26/politics/axe-files-obama-transcript/
The Bible: John 1:1

artist: jennifer hetrick, photograph, "plains coreopsis"

BOLD AND BEAUTIFUL

Bold little beauty! I remember the kind of confidence you radiate today.

Look at you: standing tall and straight!

And all by yourself, just bursting with pride, self-confidence, and energy.

And how clever of you to choose to bloom in that particular spot!

The stony wall behind you—a solid and enduring structure, certainly—contrasts profoundly with your special mission—brightening the world around you in this very moment.

And at this moment, who can refrain from smiling at those in-your-face vibrant gold petals of yours?

But I suspect you're not just a pretty face. The rich, dark center color of your petals suggests a depth of wisdom available to those young buds behind you waiting their turn to open and bloom.

I salute you, "plains coreopsis" and thank the glory of the Universe that put you in my path today.

Today my own energy wanes. My confidence falters.

I've packed away the hopes and dreams of sunnier youth. Worries and concerns crowd my consciousness along with the certainty that sunshine fades as summer's days grow shorter.

But for this moment, I will borrow your bright energy and reflect on the Spirit that informs it, for it endures forever.

~*Jane Stahl*

Jane Stahl currently serves as Director of Community Relations for Studio B following 35 years of sharing a love of literature, writing, and speaking with junior high and high school students and a love of teaching with fellow teachers and the community. Following their dream of living in an artistic community, Jane and her husband Paul founded Boyertown's Bear Fever community art project that ultimately led her into collaboration with fine artist Susan Biebuyck and the establishment of Studio B. So many projects, so little time! Jane hopes someday to take the time to self-publish a collection of her thoughts and experiences.

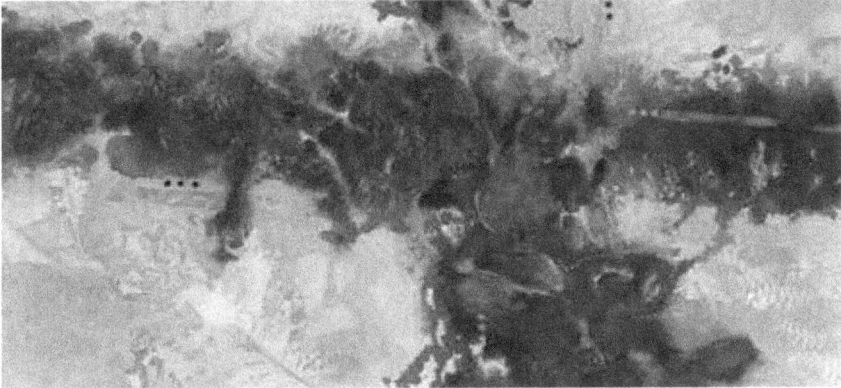

Artist: Lynn Millar, watercolor, "Fundamentally Sound"

PURITY OF RECEIPT

Her beauty is genius
Her kindness unbridled
There's never a question,
It troubles us all

The women retire
And the men will perspire
Wisdom outnumbered
And a madness recalled

A soft seldom fury by a victimless jury
Hard self-confinement through questioned withdraw
The ignorance is painted that buries us all
Nobody sins when the devil is all.

And who without wonder
Will condone your blindness

For thought of material
Has been purchased by mind

Vacation's a number
A presence of beauty
Forgotten with time
Predicted like prime

Which of you invited this madness?
Who can I blame that opened the door?
A recipe of chemicals baked once more, and more.
A fluid, or solid; that opened the door? Open the door!

A left that is right
Direction unchanged
The arrow still points
At heaven this choice

Pathways are noticed
But nobody embodied
Canvasses once painted
A symphony voiced

A language unlearned, your stupidity choice
Of linear words and letters become noise
Self-destruction, mental and physical maze
Deteriorate in instances and born through craze.

And is there a random
In the word so lost
Or a box that is locked
Only through ignorance bound.

Our masters are saviors
For creating the pattern

Reordered by accident
A genius is found

Is the pattern the lie, or the lie the pattern?
A note that is wrote, through language a sound
A son is the father, and the mother the sun
Special anomalies the children form one.

Pieces of puzzles
That I cannot solve
Doctors and lawyers
Lead to patient resolve

Artistic compression
Noteworthy possessions
A master's exhaustion
To smoothing resolve

The door is now open, and always been open
Blinded through acceptance of madness to hide
A genius, a master, a father of son, or one?
Riddles are formed of less, more, or sum.

~ *J.D. Stahl*

J.D. loathes labels, but in this "go-round" of his many lives he's a teacher, a life coach, a musician, and lover of language. Challenging accepted norms, led by logic and love and an eternal quest for truth, J.D. infuses good intentions toward the recovery and self-discovery of those whose life paths cross his own. For his own evolution, J.D. is constantly seeking ascension towards universal concepts and answers encompassing this world and the next. His own mentor is his beloved canine Ginger.

Artist: Joe Hoover, Watercolor, "Dawn's Early Light"

NOVEMBER NIGHT

It is a November night. The leaves have fallen from the trees. They cluster and tumble in waves across the ground. Gnarling tree branches reach to the sky like withered hands grasping at ominous clouds as they drift overhead. The clouds pull apart as a velvet black sky opens to the infinite.

A flood of moonlight illuminates steaming vapors of breath as they float to dissolve into the night air. Her pale flesh shimmers against the darkness. My hand casts a long shadow as it slowly caresses her volatile nakedness. Moonlight lifts the rush of prickles on aroused skin.

Our gradual embrace begins to whirl as we slowly melt into a pool of blackened silver. It ripples in the strong gusts of wind. Glistening rows begin to push across the pool with increasing intensity. Overhead, massive clouds begin to merge, and at once all visibility is lost in a dark world.

~ *Burton Stehly*

In the late 80's and early 90's Burton Stehly was the lyricist-poet for the experimental industrial group "Slavekind". In his travels he met the world renowned electronic instrument designer, Phillip Cirocco; Arizona avante-garde jazz bassist, Gary Evans; and Michael Macdonald, former drummer of the group "Gene Loves Jezebel" from Scotland. This became the touring group "National Razor." Burton was lyricist for their four subsequent album releases. He also continued live reading performances. He was never content to write strictly about personal feelings although it was a great self-therapy. Consequentially, he turned from inward to outward on the many lessons and pathways in the world he was traveling. His latest endeavor is a collection of writings in his book entitled Beauty Among Thorns, available through Create Space or by contacting him the1burton@yahoo.com

artist: jennifer hetrick, photograph, "firefly"

FIREFLY

Now that I'm getting on in years, I have thoughts of times past and the wonders of life as seen only through a child's eyes. Running through fields and trying to catch these little stars that must have fallen from heaven. So many, so beautiful, and so full of mystery. I can close my eyes and still see them, thousands of them.

I really didn't think stars could fly, but they can. The wonder stays with me to this day. Even now, I see them, and one day soon, they will come for me and take me into their world of flying stars and love.

I still see my flying miracles through my child's eyes and feel them with my child's soul and heart. Some poems you read, and others you see flying through the night.

~ *Joseph Swider*

From an absolutely loveless childhood background, Joseph Swider spent many decades attempting to make himself into a creature of love and understanding. He projects everything he has learned into the things he does. He has worked many jobs in his lifetime and has done them well. Today, Swider applies himself to a few projects that he loves—cooking, baking, fishing, and learning from the people he holds dear to him, especially the women in his life. They have so much to say, if only we listen. He lives a life without secrets, lest he become a prisoner to them. Swider owns many things but keeps in mind that which we cannot freely give away—we do not own.

Artist: Theodore Thomas, Pastel, "Woman Alone"

WOMAN ALONE

New York's parks in winter twilight have always struck me as particularly chill and gray. Barren limbs against towering gray buildings. The only warmth is the gaslight, and that's out of reach.

The view in the painting is of Bryant Park, looking west from the restaurant behind the New York Public Library. The figure is Dalia Jarashow: New Yorker, Holocaust survivor, and friend. A visit to New York with my wife usually included dinner with Dalia. I always made time to visit her workplace, the Holocaust Restitution Society at 45th and Broadway. Her office walls were papered with German Army situation maps. These extraordinary maps gave the exact position of Wehrmacht units on the Russian Front in July 1943, the time of the deepest eastward penetration of German armor.

Since the fall of the Berlin Wall, when someone approached the Society with a claim on estates, lands, art, Dalia would step to these maps and pinpoint the location of the claimed loss. If it were west of the north-south battle lines on these maps, the Holocaust Society would mobilize behind the claimant and vigorously pursue the return of the asset to its owners. However, if it lay east of those lines, the claimant was politely dismissed.

As I sketched this scene, seated in the restaurant waiting for the check, watching this diminutive widow and grandmother grow smaller in the twilight, I realized I was watching the trusted gatekeeper whose quiet decisions have, for years, initiated the recovery of millions of dollars of property looted by the Nazis from eastern Europe.

~ *Theodore Thomas*

Artist: Theodore R. Thomas, Pastel, "War and Remembrance"

WAR AND REMEMBRANCE

Morton Jarashow served as a ball turret gunner in his B-24 in 1943 over German-occupied Europe. The painting symbolizes the courage and heroism of Morton and many others of The Greatest Generation.

His wife Dalia Jarashow, in her own unique way, served in helping to restore stolen property that was taken by the Germans. Dalia is pictured in the painting walking in a snowy New York park in 2010. Dalia lost her entire family in the Holocaust and fled to Palestine as a war refugee only to be drafted into service in the Arab-Israeli War while still in her teens.

I painted these pieces and gave them to Mort and Dalia so their children would have some idea of the history of what their parents did during WWII and their life after.

***~Paintings and writings submitted by Theodore R. Thomas,
Korean War Veteran***

Theodore Thomas, retired engineering executive and Korean War veteran, traveled the world sketching, writing, and photographing his experiences over a working lifetime, drawing inspiration to create a body of pastel paintings that preserve his memories. Some have historical importance.

Artist: Daniel Gorman, Oil, "Glow"

EMBRACE THE HILLS

"Hills. We love them. We hate them. They make us strong. They make us weak. Today I chose to embrace hills." *-Hal Higdon, running writer and coach*

This is one of my favorite quotes because it applies not only to running but to life in general.

Most days when I run, I prefer to take the flat, easy course. I don't have to think; I merely have to run. I know I can finish without strain or struggle; but when I'm done, I realize I've done nothing to challenge myself to learn or fully enjoy the experience.

Once a week, though, on my workout Wednesdays, I make myself run the hills, particularly a long hill. I wake up dreading the day, knowing I will have to push myself to get up the road. I will struggle, and my knees will hurt. It will be hard to breathe, and I will want to stop. Yet, I will push on until I reach the end. When I am at the top, I stop to catch my breath and enjoy the most spectacular sunrise and view of the countryside. Few see this, and I feel special and stronger every time I do.

In my life, I often find myself seeking the flat, easy course. It's much easier to balance the demands of work, family life and activities if there are no hills. Yet, at the end of the day, what have I learned? Where is the spectacular moment of reaching the top and enjoying the accomplishment? It doesn't exist on the flat, comfortable course.

Still, hills are tough. They push me to use muscles and will power I didn't know I had, and they can be painful as I learn how to tackle them. Unfortunately at times, I am weak and have to stop. I fail and it hurts.

Failure, as I have learned, is not the end, though. It's that moment in time when I have to figure out what I did wrong and how I can fix it or prevent making that mistake again.

Running has taught me to set goals and accomplish them by persistently working at them one day at a time. When I first started running, I could barely make one lap around my neighborhood. When I ran my first mile, I felt so good I told at least 10 people about it. Now, several years later, I can say I've run three half-marathons this year. Next year, my goal is to run my first marathon.

However, I have had "failures" along the way, including a stress fracture, pulled muscles and bruised toes. Each injury taught me how to improve my running and become stronger. Now, I just need to learn how to apply this mentality to all areas in my life.

Along my journey, I realize I have two kinds of hills. There are hills I am aware of and I purposely try to avoid by seeking that flat, easy road. This is why I continue to work at a dead-end job I don't particularly like but comes with a secure paycheck and benefits instead of searching for and pursuing my passion.

And then there are those hills that unexpectedly confront me as I turn the corner, testing my resolve, like when my children call out of blue with problems, a family member becomes sick, or a house repair puts a strain on our family budget.

As I tackle the hills in my life—both the known and unexpected, I have learned I'm never running them alone. God is at my side or even carrying me when I need Him the most. Some days, the hill seems incredibly steep and endlessly long. Only through my faith in Him am I able to trudge along, knowing I need not worry. God's got this and every hill I will encounter.

With His guidance, I can learn to find a pace where I can tackle the challenges without becoming burned out and defeated. I also am learning, as I have done with my running, to set goals, block out distractions, and work every day to reach those goals and not just settle for the easy road.

Embrace the hills.

~*Diane VanDyke*

Whether she is writing a journal entry or an article for a local newspaper, Diane VanDyke finds her creative zone when she connects words and phrases to paint a lasting image and tell a good story. Her writing adventures started in her teenage years, but then were put aside and rediscovered a decade later when she started freelance writing for her hometown newspaper. Her freelance assignments led to a part-time staff position and then to a full-time editorial position. Eventually, she followed the path of marketing and public relations, where she uses her writing skills today. Beyond writing, Diane likes to garden, hike, jog, read, ride bike, and enjoy the beauty of sunrises and sunsets.

Artist: Bob Williams, Ink sketch, "Piazza Santa Croce, Tuscany"

How Do I Love Thee?
Let Me Count the Ways

While reminiscing about a long-ago stay in Florence, Italy, I decided to attempt to describe, if I ever could, the ways in which I loved that city.

After we have traveled to a new place, memories of it can last a lifetime. Many years ago, my husband Robert and I went to Florence to live for one year. We left after only a few months, discouraged and sad. Our money had run out; I could not find a job, and Robert's plan to work with another artist fell through. When I look back, however, it is not the failed plan I remember most; it is the Being of Florence—a masterpiece itself—offering rich treasures for the soul. The impressions and memories of that time, I took with me and cherish them to this day.

As young people, just married, our lives ahead of us, it was a great adventure. We found a tiny, lovely apartment with a little fireplace on via di San Giuseppe. It was across from a side entrance to the Basilica of Santa Croce, with its green and white checkered limestone facade rising in busy, sunlit Piazza di Santa Croce. From our window, we had a view of the figure Dante standing watch in the square.

When we first entered the church, I was in awe of its exquisite architecture and embellishments—the columns, statuary, stenciling, paintings, sculpture and the ornate marble tombs of the three masters of art, astronomy and politics: Michelangelo, Galileo and Machiavelli. Exploration of the art and history in this one Florentine church alone could occupy a person for a lifetime.

Every day and night was a sensual feast in Florence: the aromas of espresso and roasting meats in wood-fired ovens; the shop windows with dreamy, creamy pastries, and the power and resonant beauty of bells ringing out all over the city. Then there was the music in the language of passers-by and the calls of the vendors at open-air markets. A sculpture by Verrocchio in a niche here, or in a garden there; the vines and blossoms dotting buildings high and low.

And, oh! just down that street, the apartment where Victorian lovers and poets, Robert and Elizabeth Barrett Browning, lived and wrote.

There is a special kind of light in Florence, too—golden light falling on red tile roofs, filtering down to the muted, worn finish on ancient stone and marble, creating such color and mood that a wanderer stopping on a tiny street, or overlooking the city high on one of its hills, might feel herself to be in a Renaissance painting. Then there is the Ponte Trinita (where Dante's eyes first fell on the immortal Beatrice) crossing the green Arno River meandering through the valley from the hills—the hills, with tall, straight cypress, orchards and vineyards under azure blue skies.

How do I love thee, Florence? Let me count the ways!

These experiences live on as treasures in my life—even if only a very brief part of it, filling my heart, mind and senses again with the memories of Florence—a city alive with color, light, sound, warmth, movement and meaning—and beauty of a rare kind.

~Sandra Williams

Artist: Susan Duby, Oil, "Sunflowers: After Van Gogh"

VULNERABILITY

Vulnerability is not a weakness, a passing indisposition, or something we can arrange to do without, vulnerability is not a choice, vulnerability is the underlying, ever present and abiding undercurrent of our natural state.... To run from vulnerability is to run from the essence of our nature, the attempt to be invulnerable is the vain attempt to become something we are not. (David Whyte Poet/Philosopher)

I love these thoughts by poet, David Whyte. They remind me that

vulnerability is partly what allows us to be fully human and feel a sense
of belonging. Our tendency to try to remain invulnerable prevents
us from taking the risk of connecting with others. We are vulnerable
when we share our creations in any of the arts, when we are committed
to relationships with others, when we empathize with the pain, sorrow,
grief and joy of others. We are most vulnerable when we hold ourselves
accountable to our highest ideals.

David Whyte suggests that vulnerability is our natural state, because
no one of us is in control. We all must face the "slings and arrows of
outrageous fortune," So, it would seem we must change our tendency
to remain invulnerable and choose to fulfill our potential to become
fully human.

We are the only part of creation able to choose to BECOME.

Does the Biblical verse that says we are made in image of God partly
mean that we have the capacity to participate consciously in and con-
tribute to the creation by being creators ourselves--even of our own
being? I believe so.

The rest of creation becomes what is meant to be without choice or
consciousness: a seed becomes a flower; a larvae becomes a butterfly.
All things fulfill their nature without choice or reflection. Humans
have the opportunity to choose consciously in small and large ways
throughout a lifetime to be more, to be better, to be more whole, to
become more true to our higher selves.

We are capable of bringing all manner of new things to creation--first

through our unique individuality, then through evolving and trans-
forming which always involves allowing ourselves to be vulnerable.
There are many times when we are vulnerable through no choice of our
own. Then there are many opportunities to make the decision to allow
ourselves to be vulnerable through living fully, loving unconditionally,
taking risks and trusting that all will be well.

~ *Sandra Williams*

*Sandra taught world literature and writing at both the high school and higher
education levels since earning a BA in English and Secondary Education at
Ursinus College and an MA in English at Villanova University . She is a writ-
er of poetry, essays and short stories, with several published articles. She has
been associated with Studio B since 2010 offering various adult writing op-
portunities. Sandra believes writing is both therapeutic and enlightening—as
"if we become aware of what inspires us, expand our imagination, delve into
our own knowledge and experience, and rely on our intuitive selves." She
collaborates with her husband, Robert, local landscape and mural painter,
promoting community arts. www.cosmicseanotes.blogspot.com. She is author
of an historical novella Moss on Stone available on Amazon.*

Artist: Sharon Merkel, Photograph, "Still Life"

You Might Give Larkin A Try

Despite his having been post-war England's most read and admired poet, Philip Larkin (1922-1985) appears to me to be little read in America. Although lauded with many honors, including being nominated as Britain's Poet Laureate (which he declined), he remained a solitary Englishman who disliked fame and never attached himself to the literary life and all that it entailed.

His bio, one might say, is unremarkable and can easily be found on-line for anyone interested. He was employed throughout life as a librarian at various posts. It might be noted that perhaps a childhood stammer was the cause of his aversion to public speaking, readings, and literary honors that required a public persona.

As in any art, tastes in literature vary widely. The musician in <u>The Merchant of Venice</u> sang: "Tell me where is fancy bred/In the heart or in the head?" Do we learn preferences or is our taste inborn? All of this is to say that I rather like Larkin's poetry although many folks may find him a bit of a downer.

One critic called Larkin "… the ultimate British miserablist. The poet, who died in 1985 aged 63, was an alcoholic curmudgeon, accused by critics of being racist and sexist. He enjoyed spending time alone and had a gritty pessimism about the world around him: sometimes born of despair, other times dark humour." Indeed, the critical views get more pessimistic.

Another noted: "Reading Larkin for the first time, one is struck by the characteristically glum atmosphere that pervades most of his poems.

The vast majority of his verse is devoted to what is generally taken to be negative aspects of life, such as loneliness and dejection, disappointments, loss, and the terrifying prospect of impending death."

Described almost universally as a "bleak and pessimistic" writer, why, then, his popularity? Because, in this writer's view, he gets it right. What Larkin does, with considerable clarity and delicacy, is trace the way we respond to the character of our times. And his themes, described as "doubt, insecurity, boredom, aimlessness and malaise" become oddly satisfying as they hit that much maligned thing called "reality."

Larkin is, in large part, a traditional poet in that his rhymed lines and narrative content usually carry the reader through a space of time on a specific day. Below is a short, though, I think, excellent poem from his second book The Less Deceived (one of only three slim volumes of verse that he had published). It is typical of Larkin's work in theme and form.

> Home is so sad. It stays as it was left
> Shaped to the comfort of the last to go
> As if to win them back. Instead, bereft
> Of anyone to please, it withers so,
> Having no heart to put aside the theft
>
> And turn again to what it started as,
> A joyous shot at how things ought to be,
> Long fallen wide. You can see how it was:
> Look at the pictures and the cutlery.
> The music in the piano stool. That vase.

Both stanzas have ababa ababa rhyme. Of course he uses "home" and not "house" as the two have rather different connotations. "It stays as it was left" is so because the owner might come back, or might it be that he wants to hold on to the past. Maybe grieving its owner who is unwilling to alter things. Or, perhaps, has died?

The home is personified. It hopes to "win back" the last to go by keeping itself shaped to their comfort. But, alas, the hinge word in the poem is bereft and all that it implies of loss and loneliness.

With the second stanza all hope of [insert owner's name] returning is lost and the house is turning again to what it started as "a joyous shot at how things ought to be." But the shot has long fallen wide of its mark.

Then Larkin gives "you" a little personal tour of the scene. One can't help but feel the pathos, the sadness, of the pictures, the music still in the piano stool and finally, the *pièce de résistance*—"That vase." That vase, as with other furnishings of the room, meant in part to demonstrate to visitors the owner's taste; to show "how things ought to be."

Some other poems of Larkin's that are worthy of closer look are "The Whitsun Weddings," (probably his best known) "Church Goings," "The Old Fools," and, of course, "High Windows," my favorite.

~ *Bob Wood*

Bob Wood, writer, artist, potter, historian, and volunteer extraordinaire, began his career as an artist following his retirement from teaching Language Arts. Bob serves as Studio B's gallery adjunct and invites the public for wide-ranging discussions on art, history, and the art and craft of writing. Bob has published four books on local history,